As a director, I cannot achieve my goals without the help of creative and coura-geous writers. Pen's book is unique in that it addresses the entire landscape of movie writing as a career, and most especially encourages artists who write from the heart and strive for originality.

> — Ron Howard, director/producer/writer/actor

One thing I know for sure; without writers, we in the entertainment business are aimless wanderers looking for a place to be. My thanks to Pen for this inspirational book.

> — Morgan Freeman, Academy Award-winning actor

Pen's advice is something I wish I'd had when starting out. His words on the creative process are inspiring and useful, and his insight into the business is essential.

> — Paul Haggis, Academy Award-winning writer/producer/director

If you're thinking about writing a screenplay, do yourself a favor and hop on Pen Densham's *Alligator*. The ride's enlightening.

> — Jeff Bridges, Academy Award–winning actor

This is an insightful and thoughtful book on the art of filmmaking. Pen Densham is a triple-threat talent: writer, director, and producer... And brilliant at all three. Since I gave him his first big break, I'm proud he has written this terrific book.

> — Norman Jewison, director/producer

Pen Densham's *Riding The Alligator* provides the essential tools of the trade and leaves more than sufficient room for individual creativity. His deep under-standing of the screenwriting process is at once inspiring and empowering. An invaluable resource that is certain to become a must for all new screenwriters.

> — Robert Mandel, Dean, AFI Conservatory

Densham's book is wise, encouraging, helpful, and kind — everything the business of moviemaking is sometimes not. Young writers would do well to keep it close at hand.

> — Tom Rothman, co-chairman, Fox Filmed Entertainment

Frankly, I'd like to give this book to my execs; it's not only valuable for anyone looking to be a writer, but also those who are called upon to analyze and comment on writing.

> — Mark Stern, executive vice president, Syfy Channel;
> co-head, Universal Cable Productions

It's like getting a UC screenwriting course for under $30! As illuminating and thorough Pen Densham is as a director, with *Riding the Alligator,* he equally arouses the writer within through inspirational and educational guidance.

> — Robin Wright, actor

Final Draft's slogan is "Just Add Words." Pen Densham's *Riding the Alligator* is an inspiration to finding those words.

> — Marc Madnick, co-founder/CEO, Final Draft, Inc.

Anyone who wants to go on the journey of writing a screenplay could not have a better guide than Pen Densham.

— David Wirtschafter, partner, William Morris Endeavor Agency

I thought Chapter 11 was terrific. I thought Chapter 8 was terrific. Let's face it: I thought the whole book was great and I want to use it in my classes as required reading.

— Barbara Boyle, chair, UCLA Department of Film and Television and Digital Media

Pen Densham's *Riding the Alligator* is thought-provoking, informative, and inspiring... and filled with a rare kind of wisdom I haven't found in any other book about the screen trade. In his closing chapter, Densham writes "Be passionate — be daring — go forward." Read *Riding the Alligator* and you are well on your way!

— Richard Chizmar, writer/producer; founder and publisher/editor, *Cemetery Dance* Magazine

Pen Densham is the perfect kind of teacher. On top of his extensive knowledge on the craft of writing, he's an almost existential inspiration to those who are looking to find their own inner substance.

— Emile Hirsch, actor

This book would have saved me years! More than just another screenwriting book — it's like having a close friend in the business to help guide you through the screenwriting process from idea, to script, to sale, to career. A must-have for anyone seriously contemplating a writing career.

— Jack Epps, Jr., chair, Writing for Screen and Television, USC School of Cinematic Arts; co-writer, *Top Gun, Dick Tracy, Secret of My Success*

How refreshing to read a book that speaks about screenwriting in such a down-to-earth, practical, and inspiring manner. Pen speaks with such modesty and truthfulness about what's at the core of great screenwriting that he manages to transcend any cultural or business boundaries.

— Kathryn Emslie, director, Canadian Film Centre

A must-have for both those who work in the industry and students who aspire to.

— Karol Ann Hoeffner, visiting assistant professor, Loyola Marymount University

Unlike Robert McKee, Densham is never prescriptive in his approach to writing a screenplay — he never forbids techniques such as voice-over narration because he realizes that the technique can work in some films. He allows the aspiring writer to understand that he is describing his own approach to writing a screenplay, but other successful writers may work in different ways. Thank you, Pen Densham.

— James Hosney, AFI Conservatory Distinguished Scholar-in-Residence

A great synthesis of practical information, philosophical underpinning, and psychological counseling... as if Dennis Palumbo and Syd Field had produced a baby.

> — Philip Taylor, screenwriter/assistant professor of screenwriting, Arizona State University, Herberger Institute Theatre and Film

Any film or TV writer will benefit from Pen Densham's gift of hope, *Riding the Alligator: Strategies for a Career in SCREENPLAY Writing.. and not getting eaten.* Complete with a photo of young Densham riding an alligator, the book serves as teacher and cheerleader. Written with charm and style, writer-director-producer Densham may be the last gentleman standing.

> — Mary J. Schirmer, screenwriter/instructor
> *www.screenplayers.net*

If you've never sold a movie... if you've never written on staff... if you're barely familiar with agents and managers and pitches and studios... BUT — you have great voices and stories swimming through your head, Pen Densham does a great job of holding your hand as he guides you through the beginning stages of planning a career in Hollywood.

> — Chad Gervich, writer/producer: *Wipeout, Speeders, Foody Call*;
> author, *Small Screen, Big Picture: A Writer's Guide to the TV Business*

Amidst the tips, techniques and firsthand knowledge, Pen delivers a book that goes deeper... much deeper, addressing the full creative writing process... life, passion, joy, celebration, a full kaleidoscope of human emotions. There is no wrong way, only discovery, a voyage into the unknown. *Riding the Alligator* will challenge your creativity, inspire your mind, and touch your soul.

> — Suzanne Lyons, co-founder, Snowfall Films, Windchill Films, and the Flash Forward Institute

Riding the Alligator is one of the best books I've read about screenplay and story development. It is a must-read for anyone who loves movies and wants to know how they are structured.

> — Michael Taylor, motion picture producer; chair, Film & Television Production, USC School of Cinematic Arts

A great teacher gives us the courage to trust our own experience. Pen is that teacher. I'm looking forward to riding the alligator over and over again.

> — Johnathon Schaech, actor

In *Riding the Alligator*, Pen has created a unique survival guide for screenwriters that marries his intense passion for storytelling with practical advice drawn from his own triumphs and struggles. The result is an insightful and inspiring road map for success as a storyteller and a screenwriter.

> — Danny Rosett, former COO, Overture Films; former president, United Artists

Not since Blake Snyder's *Save the Cat!* has a book come along that gives you all the basics you need to put pen to paper, or fingers to keyboard. It's "Cats vs. Alligators" where the winner is the reader. Simple and brilliant!

> — Matthew Terry, producer/screenwriter/teacher/columnist
> *www.hollywoodlitsales.com*

BRAVO! Pen Densham's *Riding the Alligator* is a magnificent guide for all writers — an incisive, brilliant, and loving leg up to help them crack open the door to their own creative and career goals!

— Paul Saltzman, writer/director/producer, *Prom Night in Mississippi*

For many years, communicating by teleconference from Hollywood, Pen Densham's thoughtful and insightful advice on the art and craft of creating an original script has energized and inspired my screenwriting students. Pen's warm and witty words eliminate the fear of the blank page, creating instead an eager leap into creative exploration. I see the enthusiasm — Pen's approach is creative liberation.

Now his book, *Riding the Alligator*, bypasses turgid methodology to go right to the heart of the creative process, making that process instantly accessible to students of every level.

— Terry Gadsden, professor, New Brunswick Community College

An organic blend of the theoretical and the practical, Densham helps us drill down into the genetic code that draws us to storytelling in general and films in particular. A wonderful ride and a perfect companion to a screenwriter on her/his own, as well as a strong foundational text for any course on screenwriting.

— Frederick M. Strype, professor/program head, Filmmaking,
Screenwriting & Media Arts, Sarah Lawrence College

A subject that many aspiring (and established) writers think about at one time or another, is "Why do we want to write — what is our need to tell stories?" If you feel this way, this is a book you just might want to read...

Riding the Alligator is unlike most other screenwriting books I've read. Not so much about the technical aspects of screenwriting, but rather about the art and passion of writing itself, it makes for a very interesting read. Throughout the eighteen chapters, Pen Densham's love for his craft clearly comes through, and I would recommend this book to artists of all types. It's a book you will enjoy reading to the end.

— Erin Corrado, *www.onemoviefiveviews.com*

An informed, down-to-earth look at the art and craft of writing for the screen. Densham deploys experience rather than cant; he encourages passion rather than formula. Those seeking the easiest answers should go elsewhere. Those who truly want to ride the alligator of a screenwriting career need look no further than this compendium of common sense.

— Howard A. Rodman, board of directors, Writers Guild of America
West; artistic director, Sundance Screenwriting Labs

If there were one book to guide an aspiring writer/director/filmmaker through their creative and commercial journey, this is it. Pen has brilliantly drawn together all the useful tools for building a marketable script.

— Michael Peyser, producer and professor,
USC School of Cinematic Arts

RIDING THE
ALLIGATOR

Strategies for a Career in
SCREENPLAY WRITING
... and not getting eaten

PEN DENSHAM

Hi GARY
A DELIGHT To
SHARE THIS WITH YOU.
Your work is inspiring
Cheers

Published by Michael Wiese Productions
12400 Ventura Blvd. #1111
Studio City, CA 91604
tel. 818.379.8799
fax 818.986.3408
mw@mwp.com
www.mwp.com

Cover design: Johnny Ink *www.johnnyink.com*
Book design: Gina Mansfield Design
Editor: Pamela Grieman

Printed by McNaughton & Gunn, Inc., Saline, Michigan
Manufactured in the United States of America

Library of Congress Cataloging-in-Publication Data

Densham, Pen.
 Riding the alligator : strategies for a career in screenplay
writing -- and not getting eaten / by Pen Densham.
     p. cm.
 ISBN 978-1-932907-84-1
 1. Motion picture authorship. I. Title.
 PN1996.D46 2011
 808.2'3--dc22
                                        2010030432

Throughout the inhabited world, in all times and under every circumstance, the myths of man have flourished; and they have been the living inspiration of whatever else may have appeared out of the activities of the human body and mind. It would not be too much to say that myth is the secret opening through which the inexhaustible energies of the cosmos pour into human cultural manifestation. Religions, philosophies, arts, the social forms of primitive and historic man, prime discoveries in science and technology, the very dreams that blister sleep, boil up from the basic, magic ring of myth.

— Joseph Campbell,
The Hero with a Thousand Faces

CONTENTS

ACKNOWLEDGMENTS

RYAN WILLIAMS

ALEX DALTAS

LAETA KALOGRIDIS

JAY ROACH

SHANE BLACK

NIA VARDALOS

DANNY MCBRIDE

ANDREA BERLOFF

ERIC ROTH

JOHN WATSON

ROBIN SWICORD

TODD ROBINSON

ALAN MCELROY

TONY PECKHAM

RON SHELTON

NORM ALADJEM

BEBE LERNER

TERRI CLARK

KAYE POPOFSKY

PAUL SALAMOFF

JESSE DOUMA

MARK STERN

EDNA AND RAY DENSHAM

Wendy, Nevin, and Victoria — my family,
who have often been abandoned for a word processor
and gave me nothing but understanding in return.

Producer/director
Dinner for Schmucks,
Meet the Fockers,
Meet the Parents,
Austin Powers:
International Man
of Mystery,
Austin Powers:
The Spy Who
Shagged Me,
Austin Powers in
Goldmember.
Producer
Brüno, Borat,
Charlie Bartlett,
The Hitchhiker's
Guide to the Galaxy.
Exec producer/director
Recount.
Exec producer
50 First Dates.
Director
Mystery, Alaska.
Co-producer/writer
(with Pen)
Lifepod,
Space Rangers
(TV pilot).
Assoc. producer/story
Blown Away.

FOREWORD

by Jay Roach

When a story is excellent and connects as both art and entertainment, almost everybody likes it. Why? How can millions of people all share in common a love of one unique story (your favorite classic here) that originates from one person's idiosyncratic mind? When a great joke kills, it just kills. Who can really explain why that happens? We can hardly get any two people to agree on anything, so how can millions unite in loving one good yarn? Was Carl Jung right that we are all connected via a subconscious experience? Was Joseph Campbell correct, suggesting that classic stories in literature, entertainment, religion, and art all come from — and work from — the same vast, shared dream?

I have never worked with anybody who is more interested in these questions than my long time mentor, Pen Densham. The good news is, he has not sat around merely asking questions. He has worked towards answers. His philosophy of writing certainly works for him; Pen has written several excellent screenplays, including *Robin Hood: Prince of Thieves.*

And it works for me. Thanks to Pen, I made a living at writing screenplays and teleplays for several years, and through Pen, I got to direct second unit on a couple of them, which helped me convince Mike Myers I could direct *Austin Powers*, my first feature film. I still connect with Pen's ideas about story in my head when I'm directing and collaborating with writers.

One of the best things that happened to me in film school in the late eighties was running out of money halfway through. I was forced to stop out for a semester and get a full-time job. I lucked into a writer's assistant gig, working closely with Pen and his writing partner at the time, John Watson.

My job was to type up Pen's and John's thoughts and ideas during brainstorming sessions for a TV pilot they were working on, and then later to organize them into sensible, readable outlines and files. I was so naive at the time, I thought writers just sat and wrote, dutifully and relentlessly churning out pages, alone, and then painstakingly rewriting them until they were perfect. That is what film school had taught us to do. There were no writing teams in film school. Of course, some writers do write alone, but I learned from John and Pen that writing can be a group thing. A lot less lonely! In their case, the process was sort of wild, chaotic, but also incredibly productive and freeing. The upside for me was that every thought, every idea, every analysis of every beat of their stories — fantastic or just okay — was spoken out loud. It was a tremendous and rare learning experience.

I went back to film school, made a decent short film, which got me several meetings with producers and agents around town. But almost every producer or studio exec said, "Loved your short film, where are your scripts?" Scripts? I didn't even have *one* script, much less *scripts*. Evidently, people weren't dropping great screenplays into the laps of first-time directors just out of film school. The people offering to meet me were hunting for material to feed the beast. If I could spit out a few screenplays, maybe one day down the line, I'd get to direct one of them. But I was no writer. I could shoot. I just couldn't write.

So, when I graduated, I called Pen and asked him to take me back. Thankfully, he did. For the next few years, I worked full time for Pen. I usually sat at the computer while he thought and dictated ideas. He would watch over my shoulder, ask for corrections, then continue, and write and rewrite through my busy fingers on the keys.

I also provided a bounce board for him, as he tried out ideas. He asked for my opinion and I gave it to him. He made me feel safe doing that, even though a large share of my ideas were pretty lame. He usually had his own convictions about what was working for his scripts. But once in a while, he liked one of my ideas and used it. He got to a point of faith in me where sometimes he would talk through a scene and then leave me alone to lay it out on the page. It wasn't really writing, since they were mostly his ideas, but in noodling the details and the description of action and the layout, I was gaining confidence to write on my own.

I loved this process. It was a true apprenticeship. People use the word *mentor* all the time. But a real mentor is an extremely rare thing.

Eventually, Pen asked me to co-write a sci-fi TV pilot with him — *Space Rangers* — and I was off and running with him on one of my very first professional writing assignments. We did the same on a made-for-TV sci-fi movie, *Lifepod*, directed by the late, great Ron Silver. I was writing, but I still depended tremendously on Pen.

I was a bumbling Bilbo, and Pen was my Gandalf. To this day, Pen still seems like a wizard to me. A very upbeat, inspiring, generous, brilliant wizard, with long hair, a funny (to me) English Canadian accent and a fantastic, loud, wheezing laugh that always begins with a sudden snort. A total delight. One of my very best friends.

I have met thousands of people in this business, but I've never met anybody like Pen. He was like a shaman to me. A trickster and a philosopher. He is a man who loves to tell stories. He's always curious. Always seeking to link up on a level that's deeper than the surface. But he is not pretentious. He means it. As his audience and/or as his potential collaborator (the same things, really), he wants to see who you are, find out what moves you, what scares you, and how you cope with whatever that is.

But on top of all the whimsy and love of philosophy and theory, Pen taught me that screenwriting is NOT entirely magical. It's a process. It's adaptive and survival-oriented. It's practical. And to produce screenplays, you have to *work*.

Making a movie or writing a script is ALWAYS impossible, at the getting-started end of it. But it does not have to be lonely, dreadful, miserable work. As John and Pen did, find a writing partner. Talk it through. Take notes. Hire a young, eager writing assistant! Organize those notes into a story that has some kind of structure and flow. Put the main beats up on a board. Walk around and look at it, talking it out again. Reorder it, restructure it, retell it. Write it down (or get that assistant to!). Read it. Again. Then read it out loud if possible. Share it with a story midwife (as Pen calls them). Then start the whole process again. Draft after draft. That's it! It's not so bad. It can be grueling, but it is enjoyable gruel.

I'm glad that in addition to writing, Pen has found teaching and writing. The better for all of us. His deep knowledge about writing is equal to his wisdom and experience about pitching and navigating the industry. And you get to absorb it a lot faster than I did. It's all here.

If you have ever had a great idea for a movie, but lacked the wherewithal to turn it into a screenplay, you have picked up the right book.

If you have a thousand great ideas for movies — or even one really good one — but have never developed an approach to writing that enables you to turn them into screenplays, you are in the right place.

You have entered the Pen Zone. It's a good zone. It's provocative. Practical. Funny. Strategic. Effective. Enjoyable. Humanizing. Uplifting. And above all, it is inspirational. If you stay in it for a while, you will emerge a better, more driven storyteller.

Again, it's worked for me.

INTRODUCTION

I left school in England at the age of fifteen, so those looking for a highly "academic" work might want to move on.

I felt that the British school system, with the best intent for my future, was undermining me as it tried to form me into a "success," which in that system meant "do it our way." One exception was a Mr. D. J. Moss, a balding, bespectacled, and sometimes bemused English teacher. For some reason, this man ignored my hellish handwriting and my incompetent spelling and grammar, and encouraged me to keep writing because he valued my creativity. I had a dark and difficult home life with a troubled stepmother and an overwhelmed father. So Mr. Moss's faith in me was significant and kept alight a smolder of hope that I had something to say in this world, because I yearned to explore, to dream, and to count in some way.

When I was a preschooler, my late mother Edna and my father Ray Densham made short movies for the British theaters, documentaries on strange sports or on people who owned weird pets, like the woman in Chelsea who kept crocodiles and alligators in her apartment.

I was filmed at the age of four riding one of her giant creatures, a seven-foot female alligator, oddly named Peter.

The experience of watching my father using a 35mm movie camera and viewing the result on the big screen was akin to my becoming Mickey Mouse in the *Fantasia* version of *The Sorcerer's Apprentice*. Cameras and filmmaking were *magical*. I was enchanted by them from that age and I still am. But I have always considered myself the mouse, not the magician, engaged in a constant struggle to discover whether I deserved a part in this powerful wizardry, pursuing a desire that many, including my own father, did their best to knock out of me. He "helpfully" sent me to an interview at age fifteen for employment in an electric blanket factory. Luckily, the owner saw through my feigned interest in thermal bedding and told me he was doing me a favor by passing on me (and probably saving a few people from electrocution).

I struggled with my teenage creative voice, doubting it, frightened that I was wasting myself. I did sell a few articles and photographed the Rolling Stones for the local TV station. I was a discotheque disc jockey. I even sold a few photographs to national photography magazines. But with no real career path appearing before me, I felt washed up, a failure at nineteen, and so I fled to Toronto, Canada. There I discovered a country that was inspired by new ideas and supported them with grants and encouragement, a country that wanted to distinguish itself from its giant neighbor through works of art and originality. Canada had a film tradition that embraced the young.

I was making short films in Toronto in no time. I was privileged to work with Marshall McLuhan, the 1970s media guru, whose theories opened me to thinking much more broadly about resonances of communication.

I met and partnered with John Watson there. We made a great team. I loved using cameras, and he had, in my opinion, one of the best editing minds in the world. We taught ourselves filmmaking, and we risked being as innovative as possible so that our works would stand out. Under our banner, Insight Productions, John and I learned to enter festivals and aim at awards, so that others might view our work favorably. We discovered that awards became a medium of quality assurance, and they really helped us sell. No one really knows what is good.

We made short films, TV specials, innovative art documentaries, all mostly with our own money. If our films failed, we would be forced to quit our company and work for others. We struggled and stressed but somehow survived, winning two Oscar nominations, more than sixty international awards, plus medals from the queen of England for our contributions to the arts and sciences of Canada. And not one of our films was a drama.

Until I wrote "If Wishes Were Horses," my first dramatic script, I had no idea what I was doing formally. I wrote a story from the heart about a small-time racetrack trainer whose only horse was breach birthing — giving the man only a few minutes to struggle to turn the foal inside the mother before he had to choose which animal should live, the mother or the foal? I directed the half-hour film with an all-documentary crew and felt awful about my lack of knowledge and formal training. To my vast surprise the film won fourteen awards and was reviewed by *TV Guide* as "the best film of any length ever shown on CBC television."

Despite my personal doubts about my skills, the movie drew Canadian Director Norman Jewison to invite me to Hollywood as his guest filmmaker, while he made a feature film with Sylvester Stallone. This experience was financed by Telefilm Canada. Norman's career is amazing; he produced and directed dozens of truly innovative, award-winning, and financially successful films: *Moonstruck*, *In the Heat of the Night*, *The Thomas Crown Affair*, *Rollerball*, *A Soldier's Story*, *Agnes of God*, *Fiddler on the Roof*, *Jesus Christ Superstar*, *Hurricane*, and *F.I.S.T.*, to name a few.

Norman's gesture encouraged John and me to move to Hollywood where we eventually created and/or produced our own Hollywood-based movies like *Robin Hood: Prince of Thieves*, *Backdraft*, *Blown Away, Moll Flanders*, *Tank Girl*, *The Dangerous Lives of Altar Boys, Larger Than Life, Just Buried*, and more than 350 hours of television programming, including the revivals of the *Outer Limits* and the *Twilight Zone* anthologies, *The Magnificent Seven*, *Breaking News*, *Space Rangers*, *Houdini*, and *Buffalo Soldiers* under our new banner, Trilogy Entertainment Group. We did most of our learning on the job, working with other young creative companions. We often invented our own ways of figuring things out. Or we gravitated toward working pros with patience and knowledge. We only survived if we sold what we had invested our lives in. We shared a horror of having to work for others and losing our sense of freedom.

When we first developed scripts in Hollywood, we hired "expert writers" and let them translate our stories to the page for the studios. Pretty soon I became convinced that in many cases we could hit our goals better by doing the work ourselves.

I am a self-taught filmmaker. I read voraciously about the people in the business who fascinated me, but not many of the how-to books, which I frequently found too academic. I believe that creativity and imagination are valuable and treasured things which deserve to be nurtured with respect and care. It's not always something you will find in the "business" side of "show business."

This book attempts to sum up some of the processes of writing and creating feature stories that have worked for me over the years. If my approaches fight your instincts — ignore them! The right way to create is the way that works best for *you*. Mine are just one person's opinions, nothing more.

I would be doing you no favors to portray my life as either an unending bed of roses or a perpetual struggle. It has been both. When you are working on things that impassion you, the stress, self-doubt, and rejection are worth bearing. The fact that my dreams were more powerful than the pain of the process has kept me going. Despite thousands of failures and rejections, the few times things worked out and the sense of freedom to live life as an explorer of the human condition have far outweighed the dark times. And I would choose it again. I do so every day.

I am often invited to teach at institutions such as USC's School of Cinematic Arts and the Canadian Film Centre. I love sharing my hopes and techniques in as non-academic a way as possible, as one struggling dreamer to others.

As a result, I have tried to compile the book that I would have liked to have read when I first started writing and developing dramas. It contains writers' systems, short-cuts, ideas that have helped me create — a virtual digest of Trilogy's development process shared with our executives —

and the experiences of working on hundreds, if not thousands, of stories for our feature and TV productions. It also offers a touch of survivors' philosophy and hopefully a *lot* of encouragement from me to you.

In addition, I asked other screenwriters whose work I value to write something that they would like to share, which I have compiled into a later chapter. My hope is that their insights might touch you, differently from mine, and help you see yourself as part of a community of artists and thinkers.

Oh, and about my caring and insightful teacher, Mr. D. J. Moss? After our *Robin Hood* became one of the largest-grossing movies in Warner Bros.' history, I tracked him down and found him living in retirement in England. Looking backward, I could see that his encouragement in a time of great family difficulty had been the one thread that had kept my hope in the value of my imagination.

And I was proud to thank him for that.

Chapter 1

THE GOLDEN RULE

Do I have to read the whole darn book to get the secret to success? In a word, no. The greatest key to success is another word:

PASSION!

It sounds like a horrible cliché, but I concretely believe that the road to success is actually paved with passion. I can look inside my heart and measure this weird gut instinct and tell which of my scripts I folded on and which ones I fought for. I call these "life scripts."

There is magic in passion. If you believe in your work (for whatever reason is important to you), you will take more risks, bounce back from more humiliating rejections, and fight longer and harder for your projects.

It is said that "Luck comes to the prepared." I think passion makes you want to prepare.

There is a great book on physics and philosophy by Leonard Mlodinow called *The Drunkard's Walk: How Randomness Rules Our Lives* that seems to sum up the effect of chaos and randomness on our goals. What I took away from it is that life is a bit of a roulette game. If you don't stake your bet, opportunity can never find you.

What will keep you betting when the odds are against you? Faith, hope, belief — passion.

The problems of the world cannot possibly be solved by skeptics or cynics whose horizons are limited by the obvious realities. We need men who can dream of things that never were.
— John F. Kennedy

As you read this book, you have both my heartfelt support and a cautionary word. You have chosen to be an artist, and you need to find the strongest personal reasons to support the children of your creativity. If you don't, how can you expect others to nurture and raise them?

PASSION!

About 350 to 400 movies are eligible to contend for an Academy Award each year. That number reflects how many features meet the minimum requirement to be voted on and are run in a commercial theater in Los Angeles for a one-week period. In other words, *the Hollywood-based feature distribution system only has the capacity to put out about one movie a day.*

I estimate that there are ten thousand viable motion-picture feature projects in development at any one time: all busy, spinning their tales, like sperm swimming towards those 365 or so eggs of production.

HOW DO YOU BEAT THE ODDS?

Try to work on what touches your gut. Try to find a power from inside that makes even the trivial meaningful to you. The odds are that others out there will share your conviction if you can find them. Give in to your magical thinking. Fight longer, be more unique in your approaches, take emotional risks. Be daring.

Hey, look at it this way: They say an idiot will often keep trying something long after the wise man quits. And frequently you ask, "How the hell did that movie get made?" I don't know if I am an idiot or a wise man, but I know it is wise not to waste your time working on things you don't believe in and quitting on them when the path gets stony. It's better for your authenticity, for your soul, to find passion in what you do. The journey will help you develop as an artist and a businessperson… even if you don't win every time.

Here are three examples of passion paying off for me.

ONE

I wrote the original story for *Robin Hood: Prince of Thieves* after I pitched the idea to executives at three major studios, all of whom told me it was a goofy idea to think that a modern audience would want to watch men in tights with swords instead of guns. They also said that no one would want to see an Arab as a hero. I didn't want to quit, but couldn't see a solution. At that time my life had changed; my wife and I had our first child and I felt a passion to try to tell a story in which men from different religions could act as allies against a greater foe, instead of killing each other. It took encouragement from John Watson and Mark Stern (who worked with Trilogy and today is executive vice president at the Syfy Network) to help me overcome my doubts and rejections, to enable me just to sit down and write the initial story as a "spec" (a written, unpaid script that the author owns). John Watson added his unique strengths to a screenplay which eventually became one of Warner Bros.' biggest-grossing movies ever at that time. With his amazing skills at turning logistics into art, John also took on the producing leadership role during the tough physical shooting.

TWO

I pitched Les Moonves (the head of CBS) on the idea of reviving the *Twilight Zone* TV series. I was already the lucky person responsible for bringing the *Outer Limits* anthology back to TV, with its fountain of fantastic stories that I had loved from my childhood. Les rejected me three times over three years before I found the right way to make the series idea work for his needs. Going back to Les that last time was really, *really* hard! Part of me felt like a pestering idiot. But another part of me thought that the series was an American treasure and deserved to be alive for a modern audience. How did I finally convince Les? First I had to convince myself. I found a framing device, a way of helping myself make one last approach. And then I wrote Les a letter that started, "So help me Les... I promise never to mention the words 'Twilight Zone' to you ever again, after this. How about using it as companion piece to *Star Trek* on UPN?"

We were shooting a pilot from a script I wrote in a mad frenzy within fifty days of delivering that note.

THREE

I didn't know that Frank Mancuso (the chairman of MGM at that time) had personally passed on my spec script of *Moll Flanders*, the story of an eighteenth-century woman surviving poverty and coming to value herself despite her flaws. It seemed to be on track to be acquired and produced at MGM and then suddenly the project was dropped. I was so passionate that I asked to meet with Frank in the hope of persuading him to read my script and maybe change the chain of events. In that meeting, he told me kindly all the reasons why the script didn't work for him. I realized he was the reason the project was being passed on. Plus, his reasons were logical.

Three days later I tested his patience and presented him with a rewrite that incorporated all his points. Within months I was directing the movie starring Robin Wright and Morgan Freeman. It was one of the greatest and most challenging experiences of my life.

I would love to tell you that every time I risked humiliation and rejection I came out on top, but it doesn't happen that often. However, there have been many times in my life when, once I let my passion overcome my self-doubt, my shyness, my fear of being called out as a fraud... a project has blossomed.

Chapter 2

IN
THE BEGINNING

It seems a basic question, but I have never seen it answered.

WHY DO WE WATCH MOVIES?

As a writer and filmmaker I'm always delighted that I can guilelessly free-range in a constant, omnivorous search through mankind's records, experiences, legends, and sciences with the excuse that I never know what might inspire my next character, story, or script. In my wanderings I've become an unabashed (but academically uneducated) fan of a somewhat new science called "Evolutionary Psychology."

I have come to believe it gives us insight into the mystery of the storytelling process: the secrets to why certain characters are regarded as heroes, why specific plots work, even why we value good acting! I have faith that Evolutionary Psychology can help us understand the legacy and strengths of myths and legends and how to tap into our basic human life journeys to touch the audience's hearts, change their perceptions, strengthen their morals, and even help them fall in love.

Evolutionary Psychology, or psychobiology as it's also known, is a set of constantly developing theories positing that evolution has equipped mankind and all other living species with certain innate skills, and that

these behaviors have led to the species' survival and repro-
ductive success, whereas others' ancestors with different skills
— or lack thereof — have led to certain dead ends. In other
words, a lot of what we do and think has been programmed
by millions of years of natural pruning of the human tree,
and we are the fruit (of the fruit) of the successful branches.
And, despite our living in a highly technological world, we
still act in many ways like a primate that inherited its mating
rituals, hierarchical society and even the love for its young,
because they were successful natural adaptations.

We are primates that developed into the human animal six million years ago, leaving behind our monkey uncles
like the chimpanzee. In fact, the genetic truth is that we are
more closely related to the chimpanzee than the chimp is to
its next closest kin, the gorilla. Extraordinarily, we both share
more than 98% of the same genes! This fact alone makes
Evolutionary Psychology somewhat controversial. And the
sciences' new Galileos threaten many of the more accepted
beliefs and dogmas about the process of human thinking.

Darwin and some of his peers first understood the rami-
fications of the fact that many of our behaviors are absolutely
instinctual, having been bred into us over tens of millions of
years as a hierarchical pack, or tribal animal. We are creatures
whose basic drive is to continue to transfer our genes to the
future through our children.

Many of these instincts — such as men controlling the
virginity of women so that the males could believe they were
expending their resources raising children from their own
genes, or women being attracted to aggressive men with
strong physiques who could bring home the meat and fend
off those who might harm their young — may be symbol-
ized now by the male instinctually bringing his date a box
of chocolates and driving a Ferrari, unconsciously trying to
demonstrate he is a superior and highly mate-able provider.

What was appropriate for the survival of a savannah-inhabiting primate may be less valid in a considerably overcrowded civilized society. Yet these ingrained systems are not removable. We still watch boxing matches, football, or even old Stallone movies. We enjoy seeing young, human bull-males butt heads to establish the alpha male who will rise to the top and become one of the tribe's "stars."

We still mostly elect single, dominant males to be the leaders of our countries, and sometimes these males attain that place of power by sheer aggression. No countries are run by two equal heads of state, or four, and few giant corporations, religions, or countries are run by women. In general, it still usually comes down to one alpha male.

Evolutionarily speaking, we seem to have a great need to gain status in the pecking order. In fact, if I interpret the theories correctly, we humans — like chickens, wolves, baboons, and chimps — feel a powerful urge to constantly monitor and improve our position in the pack. The higher we can get in society, the more we have the food, mating, and advantages to protect our young.

In civilized life, this translates from a fascination with the pecking orders of sports (the Super Bowl) to a desire to read Time-Warner magazines about the social set of the day (Brad and Angelina have mated), or even to study the entertainment trade magazines to see which executives, stars, directors, or writers have stumbled or risen in our own jungle.

Evolutionary Psychology touches the whole human cosmos and is, in fact, too deep a subject to explain all of its implications in a single chapter. Books that have helped me understand this subject include Robert Wright's *The Moral Animal*, Jared Diamond's *The Third Chimpanzee*, Desmond Morris' *Manwatching*, Carl Sagan and Ann Druyans' *Shadows of Our Forgotten Ancestors*, and Denis Dutton's *The Art Instinct: Beauty, Pleasure, and Human Evolution*.

These books have convinced me that humankind is on the brink of discovering enormous behavioral applications of this evolutionary approach to the rationales for the human character. With nearly eight billion of us on this planet, in order to survive in the new world, we need to understand our unconscious drives that are no longer appropriate, and work towards preventing war, greed, and discrimination.

As a creator of written materials that are based on human behavior, the more I read the more I want to apply an anthropological Sherlock Holmesian deductive process to the exploration of my own spheres of interest.

WHY DO WE WATCH MOVIES?

I am awed by the unique human phenomenon of an audience falling into a trance while watching a movie. Frequently, I try to catch a glimpse of my fellow moviegoers in that darkened theater: strangely tranquil, yet unconsciously moving their faces to mimic the expressions of the actors on the screen. A "good" movie keeps us woven in its dream. We never stop to ask, "Where did that orchestra come from?" We never flinch when a character pops forward from a wide shot to a close-up. We do not ask where the characters go when they step out of frame. We do not even question incredible time jumps and contradictory cuts between images. Only in a "bad" movie do we wake up and look at our watches. Whatever is happening when a movie works, it is a weird and wondrous hypnotic rapture.

Researchers say that a child watching a television actually uses fewer calories than a youngster lying in a bed. They also say that a baby mimics its mother's mouth movements from the day it is born. To me this means that right from birth we engage in the act of gaining something from being entertained... and that something very mysterious is happening.

We seem to be willing to pay good money and put up with a level of discomfort, from hiring the baby-sitter, to traveling to and fro, to lining up in all kinds of weather, and so forth when we anticipate a good voyage into that blissful state of being an audience. I do not think it is an accident that we find these experiences fulfilling.

I have coined the name "Learning Trance" to try to define why our species loves the movies, theater, and story-telling. From my unscientific extrapolations from the theories of Evolutionary Psychology, I have come to believe that the desire to be in a Learning Trance — watching a dramatic experience unfold and resolve — is biologically programmed into us because it has been amazingly useful to our continuing evolution.

AN EYE TO THE FUTURE

Over the six million years that humans have evolved from their fellow primates, their genes have only been passed on by those who survived to reproduce. These paths to the future came through instincts and abilities in place well before the use of language. I believe by intensely observing the successes and failures of others in our animal society, our ancestors gained vital knowledge that they could employ to change their own behavior and heighten their chances to survive and protect their young.

By observing how Uncle Chimp got cornered and eaten by a lion, or why he dropped dead after eating the wrong berries or fought the alpha male for first rights on the band's eligible females, the ability to concentrate intently and learn from observation was a powerfully self-selecting survival skill.

It even explains why we slow down to observe traffic accidents; that instinct to learn from another's tragedy is bred in through millennia, and the complacent ape who ignored the opportunity to observe and learn drove too fast around the next bend and crashed on the road to the Ice Age.

LEND ME YOUR EARS

When *Homo habilis* evolved to include the persistence of oral history in his mental tools, man became one of the few beasts whose elders lived beyond the age of reproduction. Why? Because the information and wisdom carried in those ancient brains led to the survival of those closest to them. A grandfather could protect his gene investment by sticking around long enough to guide his offspring verbally and physically to the only water hole available during that rare period of a tough drought. Those who could retain information and tales that helped protect and bind the group together gained a genetic immortality. Holding an audience and the art of listening intently became as useful as observing.

SO WHAT THE HELL DOES THIS HAVE TO DO WITH MOVIES?

When watching a movie, I sometimes try to analyze my internal trance state of being an audience member. Up front, I seem highly absorbed, watching the actors simulating their emotions and tracking the story, while in the back of my head I catch myself making mental notes about my own responses to these situations. Would I go into that room on *Halloween*? Would I kiss Scarlett Johansson? Would I fight Rocky? These internal calculations are akin to mental rehearsals for possible life events. Useful stuff: I do not actually have to die to figure out how to keep Brutus and his fellow senators from ganging up on me.

Modern brain studies have recently found a possible receptor for these experiences: a component of the brain called mirror neurons. Studies show that parts of the brain activate as we watch other humans in the same areas, as if we ourselves were experiencing their acts. In other words, if we watch someone do a back flip at the Olympics, the parts of our brains that we would use if we were doing the same activity light up on an MRI. I find this even more fascinating when it is currently considered that people with autism do not seem to have these receptors.

Mirror neurons make me ask in my unscientific way: Do these unique brain cells make us experience movies more deeply than we had thought?

I do not think it is an accident that Hollywood has been described as the "Dream Factory." In one more leap of thinking, I've come to the conclusion that somehow movies, videos — stories — affect our unconscious minds in the way that dreams do. Essentially, I think that these performed stories work on something I would call our dream receptors. While no scientific source has yet defined the purpose of dreaming, current theories point out that dreams reintegrate our psyche by symbolically playing out the events in our waking life that change or fragment our personality or life path.

Using the analogy of a computer hard drive, dreams may act like a sorting processor to take the fragmentation of the day's life events and optimize us back together into a more robust version of ourselves. Essentially, dreams mimic the model of many stories. Time and events fragment a character's life, and we watch as characters struggle to deal with these new difficulties and (in most cases) reprocess the new information, make changes, and blend themselves into stronger, more capable beings. I think we view happy story endings as a reintegration of character goals. If this theory is right, it might explain why we like actors to mimic real-life behavior with a strong degree of authenticity. We gain more knowledge and reintegration when the characters' emotions and actions are portrayed as close to biological reality as possible. This intuitively feels right; it is what we call a "good" performance.

And we do like happy endings. The bad guy gets it. Justice is corrected; society's balance is restored. The tribe moves to safety after the storm. The boy and girl mate and live happily ever after. A recent PBS documentary, *The Human Spark*, explored an amazing experiment. A six-month-old child was shown colored blocks moving on a board that simulated an incline. One colored block attempted to push a climbing block down. A second, differently colored block was shown, separately, helping push the climbing block up the incline. When offered the blocks to play, the child chose the "helper" block. The experimenter explained that children always picked the helper block. The concept is stunning: Almost from birth we differentiate heroes from villains, and we embrace the good guys. Heroes and happy endings provide instructional models for creating a safe, valuable, and moral environment in which to raise our DNA carriers — our kids.

There is a dangerous side to being in a Learning Trance, one that seems to prove its existence, as we are easily manipulated when we are in this state. It is called advertising and propaganda and it works almost too well. Hypnotized, we are vulnerable to suggestion and often can end up mimicking the actors by buying that car, that lipstick, those cigarettes, that politician.

Believe me, if the ability to manipulate the human animal in a Learning Trance did not work, corporations would not spends tens of billions of dollars annually on commercials to con us into unconsciously buying their products.

FROM SOPHOCLES TO ERIC ROTH

Joseph Campbell has become the patron saint of many screenwriters. Among his works he wrote *The Hero with a Thousand Faces*. Campbell's studies of myths, legends, and religions suggest that exactly the same story components crop up in every culture, language, and historical age. Therefore, the human animal seems to like seeing the same stories over and over again, with only slight variations of time, place, or character (ergo, television).

I was introduced to Campbell's work years ago by my writing assistant and collaborator, Jay Roach. Jay has gone on to become one of Hollywood's most successful comedy filmmakers, with hits like *Austin Powers* and *Meet the Parents*, as well as his success in helping bring *Borat* to the screen. While Jay was technically working for me, his friendship and writer's insight expanded my skills, and his introduction of Joseph Campbell's work helped me find an invaluable route to the soul of writing.

Campbell's explanation of the repeating structures of myth is said to have inspired George Lucas' structuring of *Star Wars*, which made it accessible to all audiences despite being set in a futuristic sci-fi universe, with robots and all manner of creatures.

If you turn the theory that all cultures tell the same stories back on itself, it seems to prove that all stories come from exactly the same root — the most primary needs and experiences of the human animal. In an oversimplified way, I interpret this to mean that all stories are about the fundamental issues concerning human biology. That is why we say there are only six or seven major plots.

These plots include: how to find a mate (love stories), how to find food and survive (disaster and treasure-hunting tales), how to avoid being killed (murder mysteries), how to avoid being eaten (*Jurassic Park*, *Jaws*, and *Alien*), and how to dominate and reproduce. In addition, there are cautionary tales in which mad scientists and bullies become more powerful than is good for them or for the tribe and thus they fall; stories about humankind and the supernatural, possession, ghosts, and/or curses (70% of Americans believe in angels; the same number believe in aliens); and male-conflict stories in which two alpha males bash at each other and the winner mates with the alpha female (*High Noon, Rocky, Die Hard,* etc.).

Why are we happy when Cinderella marries the Prince? Is it because she has managed to engage a mate whose royal status will give her young a better chance to survive? What do *Robin Hood and His Merry Men, Snow White and the Seven Dwarfs, Star Wars, The Dirty Dozen,* and *Seven Samurai* have in common? Are they basic folk plots that encourage an altruistic, tribal heroism that defends others whom we recognize as being like us, so that "our" tribe can have the opportunity to survive and reproduce?

Why does Shakespeare last through generations? Maybe it's because his core interest is about the same basic elements of human nature and politics that are powerfully important to survival and success no matter what period of human history one lives in? Fashion, cultures, nations, religions come and go, but our biology does not change. Kings, bosses, bullies, heroes, and alpha apes still rise and fall, leading to a change in everyone's pecking order.

AH, BUT WE'RE JUST TRYING TO ENTERTAIN PEOPLE!

Yes, but we filmmakers are also modern shamans inheriting a long and respectful history: the art of interpreting human nature and the mysteries of our existence. As a consequence, in such a spiritually powerful medium, I believe it is both a privilege and a responsibility when we create. Artists are curious and pained with the gift of inner sight.

The daily grind of making a movie is like a military campaign. Filmmaking is trench warfare. To ask so much of your fellow artists, to spend so much time, money, and creativity to make a film, you should have a vital cause that moves you, a message that is compassionate and worthy. And, as technology delivers vast global audiences to interact with our creations, we are weaving human dramas that potentially speak to all the nations of this Earth. We may even be responsible for finally inducing *Homo sapiens* to view ourselves as one, global tribe: humankind (hopefully with the emphasis on "kind").[1]

---

[1] A version of this chapter was included in Lorian Tamara Elbert, ed., *Why We Write: Personal Statements and Photographic Portraits of 25 Top Screenwriters* (Los Angeles: Silman-James Press, 1999).

Chapter 3

WE ALL
HAVE DOUBTS

> *Imagination is more important than knowledge. For while knowledge defines all we currently know and understand, imagination points to all we might yet discover and create.*
>
> — Albert Einstein

YES, BUT CAN I WRITE?

This chapter hopes to journey you to the most illogical and wonderful places in yourself. And it won't always make sense.

There are no experts on how *you* should be creative. In fact, my first rule is: Ignore everything I or anyone else says that might impede your natural process and inhibit your courage to create. What works for one might disable another's inspirational process.

Human experience is unknowably vast. There is *no good reason* that your viewpoint should not be artistically valid and deserve to be shared with others.

Our geographical place in this world — our nature, our myriad cultures, our spiritual beliefs, our life experiences, our families, the accumulated data we have discovered in all the fields of our existence (and the discoveries we are yet to make) — mean that we each consist of unique oceans of information, facts, rules, emotions, instincts, and prejudices. We creators swim in these vast, unconscious depths inside ourselves.

No other human has been socialized, educated, or conditioned to experience their lives identically to us. From our individual perceptions, life paths, and genetic instincts comes the indisputable logic: *What we think, and what we have to say, is distinctive.*

EACH OF US IS LIKE A UNIQUE HUMAN INSTRUMENT

We may doubt our creativity only because we have not found the kind of "music" we are destined to excel at. Simplistically, if you are a violin, no matter how much those who influence you try to force you to sound like a bass drum, it isn't going to sound right or bring you any satisfaction. It will cause you to lose faith in your creative value.

I believe the true joy is to find what instrument you are through experimentation, and then give yourself to playing that instrument in relationship to your natural talent.

I encourage you to see yourself as a composer of your life thoughts. They don't have to be accurate, correct, in style, obviously salable, or even acceptable. Define yourself by creating from who *you* are.

▸ This is also called having a "voice," a distinctive and resonant character to your work.

▸ Creativity is a magical and shamanistic thing.

▸ Creativity should not have rules, but here is one: Be daring!

▸ And here is another: Be patient and forgiving of yourself.

Great ideas don't always come with a thunder strike. In their early formation, creative concepts are often wispy, ethereal thoughts that barely stop in the brain. They come at inconvenient times and often in puzzle pieces that feel valuable, but you don't know why yet.

New ideas are like small children; we need to encourage them, nurture them, help them to walk, talk, and to grow.

It is best to share them only with people who have an understanding and supportive nature. I call these people "story midwives." They have grace and a positive ability to provoke you to keep going. I try to avoid people who are less insightful and more dogmatic during early formative stages. I have allowed myself to be discouraged by sharing with people who do not comprehend my goals or who have a different agenda, and I have allowed myself to quit on projects.

THE SHIP IN THE DOCK

The maturation of a creative concept is frequently not a straight line. In fact, we often depress ourselves when we look at what others have accomplished. Their script, book, movie, or sculpture *seems so complete and certain.*

But what we see is the end result of their voyage. We have no idea how long it took to get there: the storms, the lost cargo, the cargo that sank and had to be re-floated! We can be unfairly hard on ourselves when we compare that finished creation with the vague little spirits of ideas that we are trying to piece together.

The process of capturing your ideas and forming them can be intensely personal, frequently daunting, and seeded with doubt and guilt. "I'm wasting my time." "This is stupid." "It will never work."

I have only one answer regarding the creative process.

JUST DO IT

We humans are drawn to track events in our daily lives and the media: our work, the weather, news, celebrities' lives, our loves, illnesses, rivals. When these experiences change, we often have an innate desire to share these changes with others verbally through gossip, conversation, or a rant! For some reason, our brains often impose a sense of order on these events; it seems to be in our nature to see life events as linked. We are all designed to tell stories.

It may be a survival mechanism, but these instinctually imposed patterns are a bonus. I've noticed that almost any sequence of events, written down, seems to work towards constructing itself into a story in our minds. The listeners or readers do half the job by bringing their own patterning instincts to help.

When writing, we frequently discover our story in a jumble of ideas and have to be patient with ourselves as we piece and discard what we intuitively feel. We should not get scared; I have often found in a script that even just jamming events together leads to some kind of sense. Nature's story force is with you.

No one can play a chess game without moving pieces on the board. Once you get into the process, have faith that more ideas and solutions will keep coming to help you gain traction.

I call my first attempt at idea creation the Lewis and Clark (named for the first two men to explore across America to the Pacific). It's a brave voyage up the Mississippi into the unknown. We must allow ourselves a few wrong tributaries, some incorrect roads, rough mountain paths, and some testing obstacles. This is all normal. It's nuts to berate ourselves as bad navigators when we don't know where we are going until we've discovered it.

When inventing the lightbulb, Thomas Edison said, as he went through more than four thousand variations, that he *"ached to give it all up."*

Creativity is work. It would be misleading to say that stress and doubt are not normal. But it also can be fun, rewarding, and truly intoxicating at times.

I believe that creativity and anxiety are similar parts of our nature. Strangely, our bodies can interpret both processes with the same physiological reaction. But artists who see their paths as challenging and adventurous look forward to the experience. The ones who interpret their journey as fearful and uncertain get creeped-out.

Try to see your writing expedition as adventure, imaginary play. Surrender to your instincts. The ideas will flow more easily.

But don't expect it to be too easy. It is a gift when it is.

WHERE DO IDEAS COME FROM?

When we converse with other people, we don't actually know what we are going to say. Rather, we discover it as we deliver the words. Or sometimes we pre-verbalize a thought in the conscious part of our brain and try to hold it in our memory until we can use it or record it.

These are acts of creativity, ideas ready to be used.

What happens when we say we "are going to think about something"? We place a concept in our mind and wait for it to pop out again, changed. It's like it's tossed beneath the waters of our consciousness into a deep, unviewable sea. Occasionally it will surface on a wave in our brain only to vanish again. Then, sometimes it seems to land on a mental beach, with each wave bringing in a greater bounty of ideas or solutions.

When we create, we encourage a dialogue with our subconscious. Sometimes the output can make us feel as if we are channeling, almost as if taking dictation from within. Other times we will collect odds and ends of ideas and then try to piece them together. There is no wrong way.

I live with Post-It notes near at hand. I write up files of my uncensored ideational bric-a-brac. I have discovered that some story ideas never complete themselves. Others come out in a torrent. And some sit in my files calling to me, but are not yet ripe.

I have read, from cover to cover, books like the Leonard Maltin Movie Guide, which contains thousands of plot, character, and movie ideas. I encourage my brain to try to mix these themes together in the hope that my mind will meld a new form. This process is called "bi-association," the joining together of two old forms to create a new one.

Jaws in outer space? This is a bi-association that could be called *Alien*. Dinosaurs in modern America? You could call this *Jurassic Park*. *Star Wars* is akin to *Robin Hood* in the future. What about *Casablanca* on Mars?

The story for *Robin Hood: Prince of Thieves* started in my idea files as "Robin Hood — Raider's Style." It was there for some time before the concept of framing the story around a Muslim hero and a Christian Robin Hood working together against an evil force solidified my creative direction. I think my vision for stories changed after my wife and I had a son. The idea of an altruistic champion appealed, someone who learned to fight for the future of other people's children. There is a cesarean birth scene in the movie, influenced by my wife, Wendy, experiencing the same process with our child.

I define my altruistic heroes as the "makers of life." They are defenders, people who find the will and courage to fight for others; they are willing to die to make other people safer. An excellent example is a fireman (like in our movie *Backdraft*, which Ron Howard beautifully directed). Firemen are as action-oriented as any hero, but do no harm, as opposed to killer protagonists that use violence as a solution to their own problems, whom I define as the "takers of life." These action-oriented characters wipe hundreds of humans off the screen and then stand with a smoking gun and a foot on a corpse, and we are supposed to celebrate the bloody mayhem that was unleashed for their selfish goals.

But, if you want to write a movie that venerates a killer, as I said, ignore my rules. It's not in me to write a movie like *Saw*, especially after having raised children. But there is a great tradition in the human arts of exploring the darkest, the most sexual and sadistic, sides of human nature in an effort to contribute more fully to human understanding. These stories can operate like adult fairy tales delving into our psychology. Heck, even Sophocles had Oedipus rip his eyes out to illustrate his madness.

After finishing my first solo directing project, a scary supernatural movie called *The Kiss*, I was asked to write and direct a much darker film by Tri-Star. It was a science fiction piece about NASA astronauts possessed by aliens who set about massacring their families. I took on the project for the money because our company needed an income stream, not because it appealed to me. The process of writing the script took four times longer than usual, it was depressing, and I would not have got through it without Jay Roach, acting as both my writing assistant and, on some days, my writing coach. His contributions were so substantial, in fact, that I credited him as co-writer on the screenplay. At the end of nearly a year we finally had a script we both felt was of substantial quality. While it still contained those very dark and malignant moments, they now managed to service the characters. We delivered the script to the studio, hoping to be rewarded with an opportunity to cast the film; the comment from the president was, "I think this is really a great script… do you think you could rewrite it into a comedy?"

IF WE ARE INVENTING SOMETHING "NEW," SHOULDN'T IT BE TOTALLY ORIGINAL?

Strangely, the answer is no. Most great ideas are evolutions of earlier concepts. It's referred to as "building on the shoulders of others." Creativity reinvents the world. Great

leaps forward are often accomplished by systemically borrowing from the best, or most interesting, existing successes
and then adding your own inner magic.

If there are only seven natural plots, then all literature
is built on their shoulders.

BUILDING BLOCKS

Once I have zoned in on my idea, I try to collect
more material that resonates thematically to build the story.
Reading or viewing materials that are linked to the concept
I am exploring helps accelerate my process. If I am creating a
buddy cop movie, I will view many similar, finished movies
(thank you, Netflix). If I am working on a historical story,
I will often refer to *Timelines of History*, a point-form book
about people and what happened in the arts, sciences, wars,
religions, etc., in every year dating back beyond the Greeks.

I will use a search program like Google Images to
visually explore themes, objects, and emotions that connect
to my goals. Movies are a photographic medium, and these
searches can return vast arrays of materials — giving me a
palette of stimulating image ideas. I often collect these in
files of visual notes. A mountaineer's rope fraying against a
rock, with a voice calling for help off screen, can be a scene.
An old man sitting in a darkened room with only his wrin-
kled hands lit can portray loneliness. Pallbearers at the back
of a hearse pulling out a tiny casket signify a child's death. A
dying soldier's hand reaching for a butterfly is the poignant
powerful last image in *All Quiet on the Western Front*, winner
of the Academy Award for Best Picture in 1930.

I will read children's versions of classic stories so that
I can quickly absorb the key ingredients: a lazy but effective way to stimulate character and story shapes. I read
and view widely, seldom copying anything verbatim, but
evolving fresh ideas that echo from the material in the way

they relate to my story. Research of any kind helps increase the materials from which your mind and imagination can draw, giving you more to play with.

WHEN I START TO ACTUALLY WRITE?

I assemble my ideas in a loose, linear form, roughly (sometimes very roughly) in the order that I see my story. One approach is to collect notes on index cards, which has been referred to as the "shoebox" method. Take as much time as you like making notes about your theme on cards or Post-Its, and dump them as you go into a handy container, the shoebox. When you intuitively feel ready, sort the notes out on a bulletin board or across a floor. It is a powerful visual and physical aid to finding and organizing your plot characters and events quickly.

I have sampled many software systems, searching for the perfect idea organizer: Mind Mappers, Outliners, Carding Programs, and commercial Plot Developers. I would love to find a simple system that worked the way my brain does. Most companies will let you download and test-drive their programs for free. Try them; maybe you will be lucky. I still make lists and use cards when possible.

At Trilogy, we liken carding out a new story as a voyage into the unknown. We call our major plot points "Islands of Sanity." We need surprisingly few Islands of Sanity to create a whole feature plot. Movie scripts are really short stories, not novels. Scripts may be 90 to 120 pages, but there is a surprising amount of unused white space on those pages. If you scraped together all the words in a script to read like prose, I estimate there would only be forty to seventy pages.

If we discover and lay out most of the key Island landing points along the way to complete the structure, it is easier to grasp the journey. Even though I have not answered every question, the work goes forward. We begin joining the dots as ideas come to fill in the spaces.

From these crude notes I write out the short version of my plot and uncritically and intuitively dump ideas into sections. I write inside this rough assemblage. *I try never to face a blank page.*

Sometimes I discover chains of ideas that might fit into several story places, and that move up and down the collective notes. I drop these pieces in where they seem to fit. Slowly, I assemble a script-like "thing," without making the process exacting or refined. This process is similar to a painter making pencil sketches before switching to the oils; it is easy to erase and change sections. I write with no effort to put it into a proper script format. I try to stay loose and uncritical: a couple of lines of dialogue here, a scene description there, a cool action beat. I leave a few other files, or sheaves of Stickies with notes, open on my computer to keep tabs on things that don't fit yet. And I try to throw away the extra ideas that I don't use as quickly as possible so that I reduce the clutter.

Once I feel I have moved from a highly mobile and fluid discovery stage to the conviction that I have mapped most of the voyage, I import the work into a script-formatting program. I use one called Final Draft. It does the hard work of formatting and fulfilling the script conventions as I am accumulating a whole script, writing up and down through the pages, adding descriptions and dialogue until it all becomes a coherent whole. Final Draft includes a thesaurus to help find those pesky words that hide in the crevices of your brain. Amongst its many helpful features, it even allows you to compare versions of your work to show what has changed as things evolve.

Even better, it automatically saves copies of your script at set times to protect you from the horror of losing your work. YES, I HAVE DONE THAT. I can still remember the feeling in my body as I hit the wrong button and trashed the only file I had of a script in progress. My body knew before my brain realized it; the ugly feeling could best be termed a REVERSE ORGASM!

Older and more allergic to loss, I email my work to myself often during the day. That action gets my valuable efforts out of my home and onto the Internet. So no fire, theft, or memory collapse can kill my project. Creativity and anxiety are linked.

This is *my* natural process. Some of my professional writer friends simply sit down and write their script onto the blank page and figure things out as they go.

HARD WORK

Once your story course is set, the process requires time and application. Scripts don't write themselves. They cannot be wished into existence. So try to find the most positive environment in which to allow this creative process to happen. Apply yourself often. I have a rule: I try to open my script file daily.

I say to myself, *I must write at least one line*. It doesn't feel hard or overwhelming. And, strangely, when I do open the file, my brain will often find itself dictating a stew of words or concepts that I had no previous conscious sense would come out of me.

It's important to put yourself in a place where your deep sea of thoughts can beach your latest harvest. Try to remove your toys and distractions. Unload the games off your MacBook. Find that place: your attic or your bed (thank goodness for portable computers). Play music. Be silent. Airplane flights can be incredibly productive for writing. I find that taking a shower often provides a strangely positive environment for breakthrough ideas. Whatever works for *you* is right!

Even in your best working conditions, do not beat yourself up if your work flow starts and stutters. I have internal weather; somehow it's important to work in the morning, but I feel foggy and find little productivity. Nevertheless, I keep myself loosely tied to the process, drinking lots of tea and visiting the bathroom more times than is probably healthy. Hunting and pecking at the pre-existing material is a common morning process for me. The early parts of my scripts will have been groomed a hundred times more than my endings.

In the later part of the afternoon it is as if the sun has come out. My mind seems to find a way to increase the flow of words. It's frustrating because I wish my entire day was this productive.

I have learned that reading my scripts in the evening when I am tired can be demoralizing. Their real values are much more obvious when one is fresh.

MURDER YOUR INTERNAL CRITIC

All writers have them — inner voices that rant and rage at our efforts. Mine floats behind my left shoulder and can be a real jerk. I have never found that voice in my head to be an accurate beacon of what I am accomplishing.

So my advice is to try to devise a method of ignoring your doubts. I have heard that some artists have an internal discussion with their critical voice. They have succeeded in damping it down by asking it to take a break until they have finished the material.

ONCE IN A WHILE IT FEELS IMPOSSIBLE TO MAKE A MOVE OF ANY KIND

Writer's block is totally normal. It just happens. I once asked Sylvester Stallone how he coped. His response was, "I just start writing anything. Whatever comes to mind. And pretty soon I find the good stuff is coming back to me."

I found this great note on the Internet one day, written by Andrew Cavanagh:

Eliminate "Writer's Block" Forever

Secret #1 to writing:
This will sound bad I know but stick with me here...

Take the attitude you're going to write ANY OLD CRAP on the subject that you can come up with.

Whatever you think of — just write it down.

Any old nonsense — GREAT. Just put it on paper (or onto your screen).

A pile of steaming crap no one would ever read?

Not your problem — just write it anyway.

Just fill up pages and pages with any old crap and keep writing straight off the top of your head for as long as you can.

Stop thinking about it and just do it.

Now if you follow secret no 1 you're going to be surprised.

The biggest mistake most writers make is that they confuse the creative process with the critical process.

When you're setting out to write something you're in the creative process.

I've written full books in 7 days.

But that can't happen if you're constantly worrying about how good, bad, or accurate what you're writing is.

You're in the creative process.

Let your creative side come out by disengaging your critical process.

If I'm writing any old crap then my critical side has no work to do. I know it's crap already.

After years of writing I began to notice "any old crap" is often pretty good.

I was using sections and pages of non-fiction writing I'd done off the top of my head over and over in other products, articles etc.

That's the first bonus.

A lot of that "any old crap" writing is good! Really good!!

But you might say "What if it's not good? What if any old crap really is crap?!"

And that leads us to secret no 2 — the biggest secret of great writing.

Secret # 2 — Great writing is all about REWRITING.

Once you have something to work with it's really easy to work it over and polish it so it shines.

It is far easier to add to a piece of writing you've already done.

It's far easier to edit writing you've already done so it flows better.

But it's very hard to look at a blank screen and write something brilliant from scratch. So write any old crap then rewrite it till it sparkles. Easy.[2]

LIFE SCRIPTS

I firmly believe that we are happiest and most productive when we are working from our true nature and not trying to guess and fake what someone else wants.

As I said, I have taken on projects that were against my nature. And it literally felt like I was having to pluck the words from my flesh to get those damn things out of me.

---

[2] For more tips on copywriting and eliminating writer's block by Andrew Cavanagh, go to: *http://www.copywriting1.com/2007/03/eliminate-writers-block-forever.html.*

The scripts that are written with a powerful sense of my inner vision are more creative, complex, and rich somehow. I call these my "life scripts." They contain something more profound that derives from my spirit, from my unconscious. These scripts are special. I instinctively fight harder to get them right. I sense that others see them as deeper and more significant. They seem to get produced more frequently than the scripts that are less personally inspired.

I know that something is going on deep in my unconscious when I write because in my day-to-day exchanges with family and in dealing with outside issues, I am slower. I am less efficient, preoccupied. I sense that part of my mind is sorting out ideas somewhere in the gray matter. And when I finish a script, I sense a change. I get my head back; I feel clearer and freer with my thinking again. I know I am done.

IT EXISTS. CONGRATULATIONS!

When you have completed a draft, celebrate that accomplishment. Print it out; feel and smell the pages. Encourage yourself. Reward yourself with some time alone with it. This is the first time you have accessed your creation. It is real.

The big work of imagining the landscape is done. Lewis and Clark have reached the Pacific. The next step on the journey is so much easier. You have the opportunity to review, delete, nip and tuck the finished piece. I call this "putting the freeway through."

I have discovered that my mind adopts a different focus when I rewrite material. It releases elements that were not needed and sees how to edit them out. Maybe I had to write them to discover where I was going. I also search out the pieces of logic that don't quite link up and try to join these pieces together.

Then I get trusted reads from people whose opinions I know mesh with my own feelings. I listen and learn from their reactions and tweak the script further (more on this in the "Editing" section).

I don't let a script out into the wild until I am fairly certain my vision is clear on the page and that others understand what I have tried to communicate. Then, and only then, do I go broadly out to the community.

IF IT DOESN'T GET MADE, DID I FAIL?

Most script don't sell just as most actors don't get jobs from their auditions. But, frequently, something good comes to gift the effort. People may love the work and invite you to write about a project they envisage, or ask to review other scripts you have. Effort brings opportunity.

Each time you create from your inner voice it is a valuable process. I have discovered that I write in repeating patterns of story that are present in many different genres and styles. When I was on the set directing my script of *Moll Flanders,* a movie that starred Robin Wright and Morgan Freeman, my partner John Watson asked me a question that floored me. "How come none of your leading characters have mothers?" I think I slapped my forehead in surprised recognition. It was true; I had lost my own mother at the age of eight. Without any consciousness I had created many stories that echoed that experience. I think that writing often comes to us as a method through which the psyche works out life's issues.

It is now clear to me that something in my instrument gets stronger each time I write. It is a process of building my creative muscles. An unsold script is not a waste; it is part of the psychic structure that is helping you develop as an artist.

THE VAN GOGH SYNDROME

Yes, there is the danger that what you create will be so unique it will not be understood by those around you.

In many ways, that level of creativity is to be revered. The language of storytelling is constantly evolving, and new visions and approaches excite me immensely. I call this the Van Gogh syndrome.

When we first came to Hollywood, John Watson and I took the marketing analysis people from Universal Studios to lunch. We asked, based on their research, what kind of movies were most wanted by the audience? The answer was "new, interesting, and different!" But movies at that level of novelty were very scary for the studio executives because there were no precedents to justify the risk. It is much safer to keep your job making a sequel to an old hit, or buying the rights to an old TV show or video game or comic book hero. Treading new ground requires courage and vision.

This is why studios are often only taken into the future kicking and screaming. The story goes that Fox Studios, fearing it had a stinker on its hands, was trying to sell off *Star Wars* to an investor as a tax break until the day it opened. The studio just didn't know how to quantify it. A similar story about *American Graffiti* is told that the executive at Universal felt that George Lucas had "f##ked him" when he first saw the finished film, a film that cost one million dollars back then, and went on to gross one hundred million dollars once it got released. In this day of corporate-run studios, original ideas are even harder to sell.

But the actors and directors are on your side. They want to challenge their skills by taking on the unique and meaningful. Look at the films that get nominated for Oscars. There is a market — it's just tougher. The problem is finding a way to define your work for the less enlightened buyer.

Sadly, Van Gogh sold no paintings but was a brilliant, if strange, man. And he had a massive influence on others. I wish you the same, except while you are alive. Please do not send me your ears!

THE WORST THING I'VE NEVER DONE!

Probably the biggest lesson I have learned in my career is that my errors of omission have damaged me far more than any errors of commission.

What I have left undone, un-thought, and untried through self-doubt have been incredible, missed opportunities. You are guaranteed a 100% failure rate if you never try. I have seldom been damaged much by the things I attempted to do or that didn't go right.

Many times I took a wild risk in the writing or selling of projects that turned out to trigger incredible successes.

I know it's not easy. I have to keep reminding myself to do it. Take on the challenge of writing… be daring!

Chapter 4

ARE MY IDEAS ANY GOOD?

There is a famous line about the film industry from screenwriter William Goldman's book *Adventures in the Screen Trade*.

NOBODY KNOWS ANYTHING!

Goldman wrote the films *The Princess Bride*, *All the President's Men*, *Misery*, *Marathon Man*, and many others. I find his point to be frustratingly true. While it seems provable that audiences yearn for fresh experiences and are stimulated by novel stories that take them out of themselves on a Friday night, we often run into really well-paid development executives who go to elaborate lengths to explain why our idea has no future.

Although there are a few commendable companies headed by people with creative inclinations, at this time, such innovators are rare. Many of the larger studios seem to want only to make replicas of last year's or last week's hit because these give the illusion of appearing to be what the public wants. I think this lack of courage and foresight is common to people who are hired to work within large corporations that think bureaucratically.

These bean counters are scared to risk money because they have trained themselves to use data and not their own instincts. They don't know how to quantify novelty. Then they are constantly amazed when an original film catches on with the public, at which time they'll grab for a piece of the praise. "Hits have many parents; misses are orphans" is another Hollywood axiom.

Maybe you can find comfort from these rejections of the famous and respectable across time: Hollywood is often no better.

Everything that can be invented has been invented.
> — Charles H. Duell, Commissioner,
> US Office of Patents, 1899

This "telephone" has too many shortcomings to be seriously considered as a means of communication. The device is inherently of no value to us.
> — Western Union internal memo, 1876

Heavier-than-air flying machines are impossible.
> — Lord Kelvin, president of Royal Society,
> 1895

The "wireless" music box has no imaginable commercial value. Who would pay for a message sent to nobody in particular?
> — Associates of David Sarnoff, in response
> to his urgings for investment in radio in
> the 1920s

Who the hell wants to hear actors talk?
> — Harry Warner of Warner Brothers, 1927

Stocks have reached what looks like a permanently high plateau.
> — Irving Fisher, professor of economics,
> Yale, October 1929

I think there is a world market for maybe five computers.
> — Thomas Watson, chairman of IBM, 1943

The bomb will never go off. I speak as an expert in explosives.
> — Admiral William Leahy, US atomic
> bomb Manhattan Project

Television won't be able to hold on to any market it captures after the first six months. People will soon get tired of staring at a plywood box every night.
> — Darryl Zanuck, 20th Century-Fox, 1946

Space travel is bunk.
> — Sir Harold Spencer Jones, Astronomer
> Royal of Britain, 1957, two weeks before
> Sputnik orbits the Earth

A cookie store is a bad idea. Besides, the market research reports say America likes crispy cookies, not soft and chewy cookies like you make.
> — Response to Debbi Fields' idea of
> starting Mrs. Fields Cookies

We don't like their sound, and guitar music is on the way out.
> — Decca Recording Co.
> rejecting the Beatles, 1962

So we went to Atari and said, "Hey, we've got this amazing thing, even built with some of your parts, and what do you think about funding us? Or we'll give it to you. We just want to do it. Pay our salary, we'll come work for you." And they said, "No." So then we went to Hewlett-Packard, and they said, "Hey, we don't need you. You haven't got through college yet."
> — Apple Computer Inc. founder Steve Jobs
> on attempts to get Atari and H-P
> interested in his and Steve Wozniak's
> personal computer

Chapter 5

HOW TO STRUCTURE A STORY

There are many theories out there. My system breaks down into three key elements. But whatever works for you is the right way.

THE THESIS, THE NUGGET, AND THE EXTERNAL STORY

THE THESIS

This is the spiritual purpose of a story. Another way to put it: If our movie is a parable, the thesis is what it hopes to teach. It is the moral direction-finder for the film.

These themes are universal, but are told through the actions of the lead character(s), and they can usually be summed up in a single sentence. *A coward learns to be a hero. A selfish woman earns emotional riches by giving her wealth to others. A bigot learns a spiritual lesson. A frightened young teen learns to take responsibility for his family in a disaster. A bully brings himself down.*

The thesis embodies a universal truth that the film will quietly teach as part of its subtext, one that could play out in any human story in any time or place. Humankind has basic, biological emotions that are valid, whether we are on a spaceship or at an ancient chariot race. The lesson should not be so obvious that it overwhelms the adventure and discovery. I call this "hiding the medicine." The thesis sets out the movie's emotional track. If the story strays from this purpose, it will seem less clear and satisfying.

The next is to demonstrate the thesis lesson through character.

THE NUGGET

I never really understood what was meant by a character's arc in drama. However, I stumbled upon my own approach to giving characters an internal journey, one that takes place as they go through the story. This makes the character change and grow. It gives actors a sense of evolution, discovery, and richness in their role.

The nugget is a simple story device that John Watson and I have applied to most of our stories. It is formed by giving the protagonist a dark and powerful life experience that affects how he or she navigates emotionally. It colors the character's approach to events and challenges.

Usually, these nuggets are best kept to one stunning event that is easy to retell and relate to, one that easily makes us sympathetic to the character's relationship to this experience. Something visceral and biological is usually best.

These kinds of backstory events are what I mean by "nuggets":

A boy's older brother died while trying to rescue him from someplace he shouldn't have been. He is now grown-up, harboring resentment toward his brother because he is shrouded in survivor guilt.

A young woman is insanely jealous and insecure about losing her lover so she smothers him because her own father abandoned her and the family.

A young man lost his father when he volunteered to go into a mine to help rescue people and now doesn't want to take on responsibility for others.

A super-simple example of the nugget in action is in *The Wizard of Oz*. Each character has an internal drive to explore throughout the movie. Dorothy wants to get home and complete herself as a young woman. The lion wants courage, the tin man a heart, and the scarecrow wants a brain.

I create my characters so that, in the first act, this negative element is in their backstory: one simple, powerful, defining, and, sometimes, horrible thing. They live with that thing, but haven't absorbed or dealt with it. In a sense, it haunts them — a failed life script or emotional program.

Let's look at an example — Adam, our lead character whose brother died while trying to rescue him as a child, operates with a set of damaged rules as a result of survivor guilt. He begins to almost hate his deceased brother, whom everyone regards as having died the perfect hero. Adam lives with the fear that he is seen as the cause of the loss and feels second-best for the rest of his life. He approaches life through this filter until the story forces him to change.

The audience can relate to living with a conflict like Adam's. They are aware that most of us will resist change. Habits are easy; change requires work and entering the unknown. It is scary dealing with the dark foreboding of our vulnerabilities. Furthermore, researchers have found that others in a social group will unconsciously sabotage a member trying to change. For example, when we try to lose weight we may find subtle resistance because those close to us do not know how the change will affect their relationship.

Usually, we hint at the backstory but do not reveal it in the first act, but we do demonstrate the character's reluctance to change. The character could be a risk taker or a scared mouse — the choice is ours. But we reveal the backstory later to show why he or she is this way.

USING THE NUGGET IN THE EXTERNAL STORY

The external story is the engine of the movie that the audience is going to see: an adventure, a romance, a thriller. Its purpose is to test our character's internal nugget and attitudes. The external story can be about an entirely different set of circumstances, but the nugget that haunts the characters colors the way they try to cope.

In scripts, convention dictates that the story is told in three acts or sections. In the first act, our protagonists do not attempt to change themselves. To cope, they just use their old persona doing things habitually. It means they will not bring their full strengths to solving problems.

As the first act breaks, the character's world falls apart (*Someone is murdered, the boy loses the girl, the rich man becomes poor, etc.*) Syd Field, who wrote a well-accepted book on screenwriting structure, describes the power and importance of the placement of the first act break, which he suggests should be around page 28, and from my experience this generalization proves pretty accurate.

Similarly, Joseph Campbell noted in *Hero with a Thousand Faces* that heroes are thrust into action when their world starts to crumble. Emotional adjustment is needed. But, moving into the second act, our hero instead just goes about trying to survive or change events, using what I call his old life programs — the incomplete modus operandi from his damaged, past experiences. When the second-to-third-act change happens, characters hit their biggest down moment.

It seems that legends, myths, and religious tales follow a universal human formula; they need to build to a giant fiasco. Campbell calls this the belly of the beast, when the main character is at his or her lowest: *captured by the villain; becoming suicidal; the girl is going to marry the other guy.* Campbell called this a "metaphorical death and re-birth with new knowledge."

Heroes are forced to realize that their past holds them back. They, or someone close to them in the story, compel the psychology of their nugget to be revealed and dealt with, before the hero can complete the final story actions.

MORE ON NUGGETS

Very few lines of dialogue are needed to explain a nugget. Its intensity should be a simple and powerful revelation: *"My father was an accountant in 1929 when Wall Street crashed. He felt responsible for all his clients losing their futures. He shot himself in a bar… As a kid I decided never to take on responsibility for others."*

Or: A young man who has never been able to overcome authority figures and bullies, says, *"Whenever I disobeyed my stepfather, his way of punishing me was to take off his belt and whip my mother 'til she screamed!"*

Now, circumstances or other players impact the hero so that the latter realizes he or she must "change" in order to complete the story. The audience will stay tuned to discover how this new persona will find solutions that the old persona could never cope with.

In our "Prince of Thieves" script: *Robin Hood was raised as a rich, spoiled child. The sheriff killed his father while Robin was away fighting a war that his father had begged him not to get involved with. Robin returns to England and leads the local woodsmen against the sheriff because he wants revenge. After Robin causes the sheriff's men to attack and destroy the woodsmen in the forest, Robin is forced by his half-brother, Will Scarlet, to see his responsibility. Robin must give up his arrogance and become a true altruistic hero who is willing to die for the poorest people and their families.*

Another example: *A jealous woman realizes that her boyfriend has abandoned her because she tried to cage him away from people. She reveals that her father abandoned the family one Christmas Eve when she was a child. Her boyfriend helps her to see that he is not the same as her father. She starts a new relationship with him in which she learns to see him for who he really is and learns not be threatened by fears from the past.*

And one more: *A timid teacher, who puts on a courageous front, is a man whose father died trying to rescue miners. He must lead a class of schoolchildren trapped by an earthquake in a BART train through an unstable tunnel under the San Francisco Bay. He reveals that he has suffered a lifetime of nightmares and panic about dying in claustrophobic darkness. He must unmask himself to the children by confessing his fear. It gives them all strength instead of scaring them. Together, they head towards the surface.*

All the above nuggets are under the skin. They are subtext, mentioned in just a few sentences in the entire script, but they define the attitudes of the characters throughout the whole piece. Be it a love story, comedy, or drama, these nuggets define how the character approaches challenges and is changed on his or her journey through the story.

This method is not the only way to establish a character's arc, but this approach has made the process easier for me, as a creator. All these nuggets relate to human feelings and events that are timeless constants in the human experience. They demonstrate the thesis. Cowardice, avoidance, doubt, denial: They could happen in any story, to any human, in any culture. Whether a sci-fi story or a Roman drama, the human animal, and its needs, remain the same.

When stories deal with characters overcoming their nugget, we feel a greater sense of completion because we have witnessed flawed people finding a way to reintegrate their selves. We have seen the lesson of the thesis learned because of the events in the story. The arc has played out.

Stories in which the hero makes no changes do not seem satisfying. At Trilogy, we have read an immense number of submitted scripts over the years that contain no inner journey. They are like a meal composed solely of

French fries. I firmly believe we watch movies to learn from the characters, and we value their changes and unconsciously use them to modify our lives.

The structure that brings out the character's internal journey, I call "The External Story." Think of it in three, incredibly simple steps:

BEGINNING, MIDDLE, AND ENDING

If we can break the components down to this basic structure, we can lay out our ideas more easily, assigning them to rough locations in the three-part structure, creating our chain of Islands of Sanity.

I am going to keep this illustration to a single plot to try to make the process as easy to understand as possible. As we evolve our stories, sometimes we find an A and B plot, two stories that feed off each other as the main, A plot, develops.

A sample B story could be a love story developing as two people struggle to complete the A story in a shipwreck drama.

Plot B can also intersect the A plot in the form of flashbacks, a device that lets us tell a story out of temporal order, a method for making the story less predictable or for making comparisons between the two stories.

Essentially, once you have determined a cohesive beginning, middle, and ending for your plot, you can artistically shuffle it around like a deck of cards to create any unique time line, or odd order of revelations that work for you. But no matter how you shape your structure, I believe that the final outcome will still play better to your audience if you understand how it reveals your character's nugget.

BEGINNING

A film is always best served if you have some kind of powerful opening hook. I call this "getting their noses out of the popcorn!"

When an audience sits down in a theater, you have the first few minutes to create an emotional contract with them, to induce them into the style and purpose of your movie. If you start with a surprise, a dynamic emotion, a significant element that powers up your movie, then the audience will be patient as you deliver the necessary expository elements. These include the setup: Who are our characters? What world do they exist in? What are the conflicts that they are about to face?

Grabbing the audience can utilize a disposable, opening element. Simply using sound and fury can get attention. James Bond movies do this. A great and familiar example is the original *Raiders of the Lost Ark*: Harrison Ford escaping from the giant ball in the temple is breathtaking but not hard-core plot.

Or we can be asked to witness an event that is pivotal to the whole movie, a compelling on-screen murder that the rest of the story revolves around. Another is a mystery that only the film will unravel: *A man wakes up with a head injury next to a dog and finds he has lost his memory and has to rely on the animal.*

THE ONLY MAXIM — DON'T BE BORING

I have taken great inspiration from one film moment that struck me as a message about writing. In the first *Alien*, the surprise created when the alien bursts from Kane's (the character played by John Hurt) chest is amazing. It sends a message to the audience that there are no boundaries in this movie. I try to include a character or plot surprise in the first act that breaks conventions. It can echo through the script and tell the audience not to relax, not to take things for granted.

After a gripping introduction, we believe in the film-maker and trust we will continue to be entertained. We'll take a few minutes of down time in *Raiders* as Indy teaches at college and we set up the expository elements of the movie.

Usually, the first act of a film is setup.

We discover that our character lives in a world that is unsettled but has not started to change in a large way, yet. Scrooge starts in his element by being mean. Snow White is plotted against from the get-go by the queen at her mirror.

And, as Syd Field states in his writings, around page 28 we complete our first act, and the world changes: *Hitler invades; our child is kidnapped; the hero loses a job that threatens his welfare; the heroine sets out from the safe world on a quest, but has yet to face her inner demons and flaws…* which will be our real reason for the story.

THE MIDDLE

The second act usually charts the voyage of the film away from the old world of the characters, to the fresh and dangerous experiences of the new one. It could be both a journey in a physical sense and also an exploration and test of the inner fabric of the characters' behaviors and emotional strategies.

The teen girl gives up her virginity and discovers she is pregnant; the hero has led his band of survivors into danger because of his ego; the poet who boasted about his prowess has lost his ability to write and now has to persuade another to write for him.

CONFLICT

The law of drama states that it must involve constant conflict, either from physical risks, emotional challenges, or both. The stronger these challenges are, the more they test the protagonists and keep the audience hooked to see the outcomes. Drama just doesn't work without it.

A superb example that illustrates the power of conflict is the daily news because it is mostly filled with two themes: (1) physical danger: fires, murder, earthquakes, outbreaks of illness or mayhem and injury; and (2) changes of emotional status: those gaining or losing wealth or celebrity, marriages failing or being announced, the televised heroics of sports warriors, leaders and their combative elections, criminals and court trials, and so forth.

We feel compelled to pay attention even if we live on the other side of the world and have no link to the people affected. It's because we are the descendants of small tribal groups who survived over millennia by reacting to violence and social upheaval. Good news does not require change. We do not need to waste precious time and resources evaluating it. But we cannot ignore the loss of our social station, our physical safety, or the perceived threat to both by others. Thus, drama thrives on antagonism and uncertainty playing on our ancient instincts.

An adversary or conflict can be anything that appears likely to overcome and destroy the protagonist or those they care about. A storm can be a villain. It can have character and seem cunning and vicious. A supernatural force can threaten to possess us. Time can be a heartless challenge. Accomplishing a goal in an impossible period will keep us riveted as the protagonist dangles over a pit with the rope burning.

Conflicts can also be about an individual's psychology, like a person with agoraphobia having to leave the safety of the home.

A boy loses his girl; a fighter loses his courage; a man fears he is too old to be valued; an innocent is accused of a crime; a group must remove its leader who has become insane.

In the second act our characters confront conflicts, and may seem to gain a little leverage by using their old behaviors. But they have not grown and adapted to the new tasks set by the story and may be stacking up errors that will bring payback and downfall.

ENDING

The time has come for the "belly of the beast," the hero's metaphorical death. Our protagonists have *not* learned their lessons, and this failure brings on a massive downfall. All hope is lost. The depth of this psychic death and the misery and damage it causes the character helps to power up the last stage of the ending, the comeback.

Then comes the final act of courage, the final test that the heroes must now pass by changing themselves with, to use Campbell's term, "their new knowledge."

Up to now they have been bound tightly by their old damaged life rules, like a snake trapped in a dead skin. Some are not aware that psychological freedom is possible; others are too afraid of change to try to escape. The hero's crisis forces them to choose, shed their old skin, and throw off their mental bindings, or fail forever.

RAW HUMAN

I describe this final phase as the heroes becoming "raw human." They must reinvent themselves in a hurry if they have any hope to complete the story's quest, exposing their raw, untested selves to the story's final tests. This adds a unique dramatic fascination to the last act's convulsions; neither the newly raw character nor the audience is quite sure if they can succeed in changing, or sure of *who* they will become in the process. But they must stake everything on this unknown.

A coward must find courage; a man must give up his jealousy to truly show his love; a mother allows her children to discover their own strengths instead of smothering them.

Endings are at their finest and most potent when they feel like "the eye of the needle" for the main characters — an almost impossible task is presented that results in a tumultuous tsunami of emotions or physical actions, or both. My partner and I nicknamed this "the orgasm."

Movies that end in a physical convulsion can be Rocky Balboa fights, action movies with battles, *Star Wars* with shoot-outs, races to the finish line — or love stories in which the hero makes a great sacrifice to finally win over a potential mate. A film can also complete with pure emotion by having the hero make a noble, public statement that is so powerful and courageous that his or her world is changed.

When your ending is explosively potent it can give the audience a sense that the entire story was powerful and successful.

The final trick is: Finish the story as quickly as possible. Get the audience out of the theater and give your movie the best salute it can have: positive word of mouth.

Chapter 6

ROLES STARS WILL WANT TO PLAY

I am convinced that actors with creative intelligence want to play roles that challenge their artistic instincts. While Mel Gibson succeeded as an action hero in the *Road Warrior* and *Lethal Weapon* movies, he also wanted to play Hamlet.

SOME CHARACTER TOOLS

When stars commit to a movie in Hollywood, it is frequently the reason the film will get financed. No imaginative person wants to do the same thing over and over. Yet studios offer stars the same type of role over and over. The assumption is that this is the persona the actor wants to play or this is the persona that the studio thinks will sell.

But the big secret is: The studios are *competing against each other* for these artists. Stars are one of the main, shiny baits for the audience from which the studios hope to profit. And to attract those stars screenplays are the bait the studios need: great stories with great roles. Dustin Hoffman won an Oscar for playing an autistic person in *Rain Man*. Forest Whitaker won playing a bizarrely charismatic dictator in *The Last King of Scotland*. Charlize Theron won for the role of a dynamic and demented female killer in *Monster*. Sean Penn won for his deep and charismatic portrayal of Harvey Milk, the first openly homosexual politician in America.

So how do we, as writers, create complex characters that will attract talented performers? Personalities whose emotional palettes are less obvious, more engaging, or totally tantalizing chances for stars to refresh their instincts and create a unique human portrait?

Humans come with such a vast lexicon of traits there is virtually no wrong way to portray our species. But, when we start to sketch out our protagonists and antagonists, we might see them as types before we see them as people. This often happens to me, so to break the mold I struggle to free my thinking and deepen my originality and authenticity.

I ask myself questions. Who would be the least obvious, most unusual character to take on this challenge? What would be the weirdest world to place my favorite character types in, thus making their behavior fresh? What eccentricity, or handicap, or permutations of personality would make a dull person fascinating?

I use bi-association, taking two or more contradictory human types and forcing them together: *A prostitute must become a detective. A fireman decides to sing opera. A teacher must become a knight. A dog transfers into a man's body. A nun has a sex change.* Crashing types together can create weird or wonderful discoveries.

I have made lists of examples of human attributes and emotions and tried to divine ideas by running these options through my mind: employed/loafer; introvert/extrovert; gay/straight; bigot/saint. (See Chapter 16.)

I will confess to spending hours just trolling through the Internet and looking up odd things like "the worst human beings in the world" or "ten things I love about my friends." I also like to read psychologists' case studies. They are remarkable documents of human experience, and can be filled with day-to-day anecdotes from real people that can open our own minds to new possibilities that will color or shape a character type into someone surprising and real.

I often review the five stages of grief, as discovered by Doctor Elizabeth Kubler-Ross, to see if they can help me create realistic character behavior. Elizabeth decided to study people who had terminal illnesses to try to bring comfort and understanding to both the dying and those who were about to lose a loved one. She discovered a set of innate emotional stages that seemed constant and necessary in helping someone deal with loss and grief.

DENIAL – ANGER – DEPRESSION – BARGAINING – ACCEPTANCE

They represent a road map to piecing together truthful responses we as fiction writers need to give authenticity to our characters' reaction to loss or damage or change. *A romance breaks up. Someone stole their treasure. Their leader has been killed.* We can add complexity as our characters try to cope with their circumstances, deny them, curse them, try to push them away... and then go on to acceptance.

This is human nature in action. It can make a fantasy or science fiction story more believable, too. Take a character who is haunted by a ghost or abducted by an alien. No real person would just accept either of these scenarios as an instant reality. We can use some or all of the five stages to take the audience with the character through the layers of rejection of a phenomenon to the ultimate belief in its actuality.

When I am exploring new ideas with that strange mixture of hope and fear, I tell myself it is important to be playful, to write as explorations and inventions — let the consequences fall later. I sometimes doubt whether all this research is procrastination and I should punish myself, or if this is valuable time when I am feeding my unconscious to kick out more complex and intriguing human amalgams. Although I do have a masterful relationship with procrastination, I mainly come down on the data bank side.

CREATE A WELCOME IN YOUR HEAD TO ALLOW YOUR CHARACTERS' PERSONAS TO SPEAK

Surrender to them. Let their voices float through you. Great writing can feel like you are channeling, taking dictation from your inner spaces. My channeled observations of humanity seem to be colored by pains or hefty emotions from my own past. I find that channeled writing is more poetic, insightful, aware of the human condition.

Do not let your internal critic nag you into drawing lines of right or wrong. Do not question how weird, contradictory, crude, or bad the material is. I have discovered that my brain is mostly incapable of making a judgment call on quality while in the process of writing. My mantra stipulates that no one will ever read the work unless I choose to share it. The idea is to free myself so that idiosyncrasies can arise. Fascinating characters are not developed by following rules but by breaking through our limitations.

Later, I am often surprised how good — even excellent — the writing really is. When you free yourself to write your characters from the heart you are expressing your original voice. It will have an imprint, a uniqueness, a potency and complexity that other artists will hopefully sense and use to bring their own skills to a higher level.

Once I have discovered my characters, I firmly believe that they must grow and change as the story evolves. Artistic actors usually work out their own backstory, an internal monologue for the people they play. They get pleasure from filling in the personality, habits, and emotions of their roles. The nugget approach provides a deeper solution to generating this emotional evolution, creating a core of powerful emotional logic that the actor can build on.

I was lucky enough to write a character called Hibble in my *Moll Flanders* script that was unlike any role that Morgan Freeman had ever played. A black concierge to a madam in a London brothel in the 1700s, Hibble had a rich backstory, having been the madam's lover once and now tied to her because she knew things that could get him hanged. When facing the possibility of casting the film, I was pretty much an untested director and needed stars or MGM was not going to finance the movie.

I asked myself, who would I like to work with? I had an epiphany. I had met Morgan on our *Robin Hood*, and found him to be a great artist and a deeply caring man. My partner John forwarded Morgan the script. And I can still remember taking his phone call. I was fully prepared for a polite pass. But... my heart thumping, I heard Morgan speak. "I think your words are poetry. I would be honored to speak them. You can tell people you have Morgan Freeman." It was the call that started me on the journey that got *Moll Flanders* made.

Chapter 7

WE CAN'T
HAVE HEROES
WITHOUT 'EM

The purpose of the villain is to create conflict that defines the hero. A "weak" villain who is little challenge to your protagonist diminishes the scale of the hero's triumph. As I like to say, nobody would remember David from the Bible if Goliath was five-foot-six!

VILLAINS

We're always going to hate baby killers, rapists, and the criminally insane, but these types are often only of limited story value. They are not complex. The most successful villains are insidious characters whose goals we can understand and privately envy or aspire to in some aspects.

Even monsters can be more fascinating if we give them emotions. King Kong perhaps best represents a creature whose feelings we come to equate with our own, creating a strange and compelling bond.

Simplistically, who wouldn't want to be all-powerful and super rich, to have sex on a whim, to believe our own intelligence is so superior that others should be pushed aside or subjugated because we claim the right to feel more important? It is said that the best villains must be heroes in their own eyes.

But when the villain's systems are carried to their logical outcome they are seen for what they are: performances of cruelty, deception, and immorality. Their greed, aggrandizement, or desire to punish threatens our future, our children, our health, or our most vital moral sensibilities. Snow White's stepmother truly believes she deserves to be "the fairest one of all" even if it leads to child murder.

Sometimes the rise and fall of these characters can be sufficient to propel the complete purpose of a movie, a cautionary tale with a negative protagonist such as Jekyll and Hyde or Bonnie and Clyde, even Macbeth.

All in all, anyone who uses their strengths — physical, financial, or spiritual — to betray weaker humans makes a good villain.

As writers we may be requested by Hollywood to write a stereotype of evil and find ourselves in the precarious position of needing to portray a villain who might represent a larger community that would be offended by being portrayed as universally evil: a religion, race, or nation. To keep some equilibrium, if these kinds of villains outwardly espouse the group's goals, but inwardly are misleading their own people and using the group's values as a cover for their own immoral gains, then the represented group can be immunized, and shown as moral and glad to be rid of the villains.

For example, a terrorist betrays and kills a moderate who wants peace. The terrorist then displaces the moderate for his own financial gain. Another example: A military official with ambitions to become a dictator is revealed to have shot down a plane full of his own leaders, having faked the attack so that he could blame it on the United States. All of these villains would be worthy of their respective social groups desiring to see them defeated.

To be effective bad guys should discover the heroes' weaknesses and bring out the failings of their nugget. Heroes should be deeply humbled, publicly embarrassed, or physically or emotionally tortured to the point of quitting by the greater skills and strengths of the villains and their supporters. We have to get to a point where we feel that the hero can fail.

I call these "accumulated humiliations." I find that re-peating a failure three times in a movie, with the outcomes getting worse each time, can build up a coiled spring of aggression in the audience towards the villain.

The first time, the good guy hero is humbled and warned away. The second time he is deeply humiliated and damaged. The third time, in the last act when the hero returns for more punishment, it must seem almost suicidal.

It is best if the hero's third attempt seems like he is being ground to pulp before his new raw persona finally clicks in and "won't take it any more!"

Whether the hero is fighting symbolically — against a corrupt politician or a clique of witchy schoolgirls — or phys-ically against a violent foe — this repressed anger is released by the hero finally kicking a## and the audience's rooting instincts reach full flush. We seem to crave the satisfaction of a big, personal payoff by identifying with the underdog as he or she overcomes a hefty adversary. We get an almost electric release of aggressive pleasure.

The world needs a steady supply of reinvented villains. They will use the old motives: greed, power, sex. The bully in the neighborhood is not going to disappear. Nor will the dictator. But the scale and methods of their plans will sym-bolize many of the new questions we face in our fast-moving, technological culture. So let your inner instincts go. What are the most greedy, selfish, egotistical, and aggrandizing things you would do if there was absolutely no guilt involved and no recourse coming?

You are building a villain we can all love and hate.

Chapter 8

NOW YOU HAVE A FIRST DRAFT

I've written a
whole script!
Congratulations,
you finished
your first draft —
now what?

EDITING

I love this part of the process. It's usually easier.

After all the effort of origination, I firmly believe that it is vital to stay the course and put our best foot forward to make our buyer's first read the strongest and easiest possible.

Let me illustrate this with a joke.

Why do mice have such small balls?
Because so few of them dance.

Huh? Well, put it this way: Like a joke you have never heard before, a first read of a script is the most potent. The unheard joke's punch line is fresh and dynamic, so it triggers your sense of humor. Once you have heard it, the spontaneity is gone. The dynamic is lamed.

Why do mice have such small balls?
Because so few of them dance.

The second time around. Dull...

The same thing goes for scripts. It is a higher hill to climb to catch a wave of enthusiasm off a rewrite and a second read. So it's best to create the most positive impression right out of the box.

How? I have struggled to understand how to improve my scripts so that others see them with the same passion and sense of discovery that I feel when I write them. I've come to the conclusion that writing mostly comes in layers, and the deepest definition of a script comes from a process of etching and chipping away.

LENGTH IS ALWAYS AN ISSUE

Do you need that many pages to tell your story? I guarantee you, 90% of your readers will look at your *last* page first: 135 pages — Oh noooooooo!!! In Hollywood, creative executives may go home with up to a dozen scripts on a weekend. These great works of ours come between them and the rest of their lives. I jokingly refer to my scripts as the enemy of the reader. How do I make them kinder, sweeter, more pleasant on the eyes and brain, and, shorter?

SOME BASIC THOUGHTS

When we write we frequently see our own page so often that we unconsciously speed-read it. I think our brain is trained to record "new" things and then play back micro memories rather than re-analyze each time we view it. The best proof for me of this odd time distortion is the feeling we have when we drive somewhere new or watch a movie for the first time; the journey, or movie, always seems to take longer when they are first experienced.

I believe this is because we are paying much more analytical attention to this new event. Once we have experienced a journey, a film, or a script, the next view always seems much faster. Who hasn't found themselves daydreaming during their trip home without really noticing the trip? We're navigating on memory.

I worry that writers and directors can get trapped by the "familiarity of memory" problem, and misjudge the reader's or viewer's reaction to their material. To us, the creators, our work seems slick and fast, but we are playing back a memory like a stone skipping across the surface of a lake. But the uninitiated first-timers have to swim their way across, and their experience is much slower for it.

EDIT AND PACE FOR THAT FIRST SLOW READ

Every word that you can get off the page and every frame that you can take out of your movie makes it closer to the feel that you experience as its author. Words in a script are like sandbags in a hot air balloon. Every one that you can toss overboard lets your project rise faster and soar higher. It brings your best ideas closer together, makes the work tighter and more exciting. It turns wine into cognac (well, not quite).

I read my scripts both on the computer screen and also on paper. I find I see things differently each way. And I have learned to make notes on scripts with a red pen. The color jumps off the page when you try to find the notes later — anything to make the job easier.

Okay, so if we misread our own work, how do we see it the way a new viewer would? One obvious way is to put it aside and let time wipe away some of your memories. Your delayed read is fresher and your perceptions sharper. You can perceive your mistakes, over-elaborations, clunkers, and genuine gems more easily.

A quicker trick I use to overcome my mind's familiarity is to change the font (type style) of my script. In doing so, the entire layout changes and brings the words to me in fresh places on the page. The goal is to shock your eye into catching the words because they stand out again (it's easy to change the font back later).

Another trick I use to trim my script is simply to concentrate on analyzing the script in a contextual manner rather than seeing it as a whole. In this way I look at just my dialogues, for instance. Or I review only my descriptions. Our minds adjust to this sense of focused editing and become very adept at spotting edits and improvements more easily.

In the case of dialogue, I have observed that on an early draft I am often unconsciously writing to discover what my story is about. Frequently my dialogue is overwritten and sometimes very obvious at this stage because my brain was laying it down like a foundation and not as an end result.

Early dialogue can often result in a declarative sentence followed by supportive ones of the same concept.

"I am so angry with you. I could punch a wall. You let me down again."

Each sentence helps the other but nothing reveals more than the first statement.

Look at just your dialogue lines and say to yourself, "How much of this do I need to make my point?" I find I can often drop the declarative first statement and make my point with little adjustment to what remains.

"I could punch a wall. You let me down again."

We should always be *escalating* an audience's interest in a scene. In this case the dialogue never gets stronger than "I could punch a wall." Maybe it means that we should switch the weaker idea first? Maybe even *act* the idea rather than state it?

"You let me down again." He punches the wall.

Another trick when playing with your dialogue is keeping the reader's attention by not revealing everything, but making them pay attention to discover what the character intends. Make the reader decode the stakes rather than leaving them feeling like the lines hit them on the nose.

"Always? Why?" He punches the wall and stares hard at his companion.

Remember, actors like to do the work of carrying the emotions, too. They are capable of giving intentions, emotions, and context with just body language and facial expressions.

Try this form of dialogue-only editing as a game. Our personal habit patterns leading to obviousness and wordiness get easier to spot and tweak. You still have your original draft. So experiment. You have nothing to lose but unnecessary length itself.

My next method to tighten a script is to run a review of just the beginnings and endings of scenes, and ask, "Can I start further into the scene or cut out earlier? Can I eliminate any presentational fluff or unneeded exits without harming the hard purpose of the scene?" The mind sometimes has to write ways into scenes to discover our story. It can be liberating in editing to cut in deeper and cut out early.

For instance, we might have written a scene in which a character asks the girl to go to the dance with him. But, if we have written that she says "yes," we have given up impact and discovery; we made the next scene obvious before we get there. It would be better to cut out before the question is answered and let the audience discover the couple in the act of dancing as the next cut. These kind of impacting deletions involve the viewer. As a director, we are always up against budget and time. Conventional wisdom instructs us to shoot the heart of the scene. It is the only part needed to tell the story. Truthfully, that is all we need on the page.

I often run my character's incoming dialogues over the visual end of the previous scene. When appropriate, this also speeds up pace and glues the story tighter at the same time.

REVIEWING THE SCENE DESCRIPTIONS

For me, scene descriptions are not just a place to list objects, settings, and movements as in a laundry list. They are an opportunity to deepen character and emotion. I am in a school of writers that wants the descriptions to have the narrative power and pungency of poetry. I like to find creative ways to describe a character's thoughts: "His gut churning with fear… our hero reaches for the glinting knife."

Shane Black goes even further; although a wonderfully terse writer, he wills us to see his vision by talking to us from the page.

This is from the original *Lethal Weapon*:

"Pats his jeans… Realizes his wallet has flown free during the fracas. Scoops to retrieve it from its resting place on the sand, where it lies open, and as it lies open, yes, folks, that is a badge we see. Riggs, we realize, is an officer of the law."

I CALL THIS "FUSION" WRITING

We are fusing emotions and descriptions. As writers, I believe we are artists, and any intuition we have to strengthen our work is fair game. You have a right to make your work compelling. Write dialogue in the descriptions if it feels right. Write the descriptions as poetry: whatever works to keep the reader impelled on your journey. Please, do not laundry list the contents of the room!

Unshaved, unkempt, unsavory, our hero lives in an apartment that looks blasted with the shambles of his life.

is a lot more powerful than…

Our hero looks rundown and unwashed. His apartment is small and untidy.

ANOTHER ECCENTRIC HABIT OF MY EDITING STYLE

I go through the entire script muttering to myself, "No dead time!" I scan for extra filler beats of plot, dialogue, and verbiage that slow the tempo. I am trying for a nonfat script.

By nitpicking and eliminating padding, the work becomes all muscle, hopefully gripping tighter on the imagination of the reader.

CASTING THE FINAL SPELLS ON THE READER

I try to lay out the script so that the white space is balanced to the eye and helps the read flow. I will CAPITALIZE things that I want EMPHASIZED. And I will double-space in a paragraph before a sentence that has an important new concept. I am about the effect of *reading*, not the rules of writing etiquette.

Also, to make a read flow better I prevent my sentences from hanging **over**.

Like the word above. Every time a line breaks with an extra word or **two dangling,**

... our eyes make wasted moves.

I go through my work and cheat the margins slightly or rephrase the sentences to prevent every avoidable hang-over.

PAGE TURNERS

Finally, I make a run through the script to adjust the end of each page so it is the most opportune reading transition. I even try my best to have the end sentence contain a dramatic moment that helps intrigue the reader to want to flip the page to discover the outcome. But if I can't find a dramatic beat, I at least make sure that the page change does not damage the read.

This may seem an awful lot of work, but we have overcome all kinds of obstacles and invested a piece of our souls in these pages. The effort deserves to be the best it can be for those minutes that it is in your buyers' hands.

So... I am pages shorter, the script is more dynamic. Now what?

Let your story midwife read it. Remember, we define a story midwife as a friendly, caring reader who will encourage you while pointing out the elements in your script that have problems with clarity and other issues.

A story is like a set of stepping stones crossing a stream. Each one should be placed with creative logic to help the audience along. Your story midwife can help you to see where — even though things make sense to *you* — you are missing a step for the reader and dropping your audience in the water.

If you are giving notes to your friends as a story midwife, please remember to front-load the compliments. Celebrate the things that you love before getting into the critiques. It reassures and opens the receptivity of the writer. Hearing only the problems can be depressing.

At Trilogy, we have evolved a colorful term for making everything really clear. We call it "A##hole Proofing." You have no idea how distracted your readers will be, or if they are a lazy a##hole. It is your responsibility to protect your work by getting your points across emphatically. A reader who missed a stepping stone or two and fell in the stream can have a wet and angry opinion! An amazing difference can be made with a script's success when the work simply makes sense.

Lastly, at Trilogy we make a big fuss about two things. It is a matter of pride, but it can save a lot of time and chaos if you are writing under production pressures:

1. If we deliver a printed script, we insist that the person who printed it inspect and make sure it contains every page.

2. If we email a script, WE DON'T CONSIDER IT DELIVERED until we have phoned or emailed the recipient to confirm that it is not in a spam filter and the file can be opened.

Develop this habit. For a script rewrite to go astray during production — when hundreds of thousands of dollars a day are being spent — is more than embarrassing. It makes you the a##hole... maybe one with no job.

A good test-read at a table with actors or even friends can bring some valuable insights, and just hearing your words voiced can charge your emotional batteries. However, be prepared for some surprises.

I vividly remember Robin Wright and Sean Penn and several wonderful actors reading an early draft of my Houdini feature script. As I heard my own words coming back to me, I realized that my dialogues were incredibly long-winded! They had zipped elegantly inside my head but, when spoken, seemed to labor like a car trying to climb a steep hill. The longer the read went on, the more uncomfortable I became. I honestly could not wait to prune the living daylights out of the thing. The Slim-Fast version of my *Houdini* project eventually got made, with the TNT network treating it as a feature film and giving me total creative control as director (as long as I was on budget).

Once you have fine-tuned your script and have received good feedback from those you trust, you are ready to face the challenge of giving your work to the world to see if you and it can find common ground.

Go for it!

Chapter 9

ENTERING
THE JUNGLE

I receive a daily flow of unsolicited submission inquiries among my email, dozens, at times. I realize I must be on lists somewhere on the Net. I'm forced to ignore almost all of them. I am not callous, just overwhelmed.

SELLING

So how do you get a script to a producer like me?

The best way is through personal recommendation. If someone I know or value likes your work enough to approach me with it, or is willing to lend his or her name to your approach, it would help to catch my attention. Who would I value? Another professional who has an understanding of the business. A writing coach. A film school professor. Another producer. An actor with whom I have worked. A personal friend. A development executive.

All have been routes to me reading submissions.

BUT WHAT IF YOU ARE NEW AND TRYING TO BREAK IN?

You have to use the same imagination and passion that you applied to writing your work to the task of finding a route to getting it read.

You must keep exploring and making inquiries. Use tools like the IMDb website to look up talent who have consistently directed or produced material that is in the mood and style of your work. Judge your targets by their body of work — try to figure out where they have been artistically and describe your work as where they will want to go. Find actors who have their own production company; they will be more open to approaches.

I have read scripts because the inquiry note was really personal and touched me. I am more likely to respond to a letter from someone who has taken the time to research our company and myself and can cite why their material could appeal to me. I am less likely to respond to a generic exploratory letter or email. I will assume that too many people have seen the material and if it were any good it would probably have sold.

Create a strong conceptual description and send it with your inquiry letters to the people you would value reading your work. Expect a high rejection quota.

Before any professional can read your script, because of the fear of lawsuits and, to some degree, to filter out the extreme amateur, most companies and producers will only accept scripts submitted three ways:

1. From the writer's lawyer.

2. Directly from writers after they have signed a professional rights release (usually intense and very protective documents).

3. Or from the best and most usual source: agents and managers.

AGENTS AND MANAGERS

"You can take all the sincerity in Hollywood, put it in a flea's navel, and still have room left over for three caraway seeds and an agent's heart." That assessment was by Fred Allen, a long-ago Hollywood entertainer. Some grimly fear that his sentiment is still valid today.

I have met a handful of agents deserving Fred's estimate of their pulmonary apparatus. But most I find are caring allies and can be clearheaded advisors because they retain a perspective that we will never have as a creator.

People in our business are wary of inexperienced writers. Having an agent or manager is a Good Housekeeping Seal. It implies quality and knowledge. This business is an ecosystem that, viewed from afar, seems to work on one set of logics. Yet when you are in it, you realize that many of those perceptions are misunderstandings, or Hollywood public relations bull. Your representation knows the game and will read between the lines of people's comments and share the cumulative knowledge of the firm.

A lot of writers feel that getting represented by an agent or manager is equivalent to finding the holy grail, the end of a quest, an all-powerful solution to selling their work. They target achieving representation and then think they can just hand over their career to the all-knowing Oz. And when things don't work out, they fire their representative and move on to seek another Oz.

I have a different perception. Your career is always your responsibility. An agent or manager is a tool, hopefully a helpful, caring tool. But you should never totally give over your hopes, dreams, and work to any sales representative and retire into the background.

WHY NOT? HERE'S THE MATH:

You spend 100% of your work time thinking about your career and goals. If you were to be taken on by an agent or manager, you must divide the time this person can dedicate to your welfare by the number of clients she or he has to service. That is, if your new agent has fifty clients you are one-fiftieth of his or her time, compared to 100% of yours. This is not a good equation.

The solution? Regard your sales representative as a ticket to the industry, while *you* work towards defining your destinations.

An agency or management firm is a great source of information and scuttlebutt on the daily commerce and conventional wisdom of the business. You can use that information when making deals or looking for ideas regarding who is buying and how to approach these contacts.

But it is still best if you do your own homework, read the trades, *Variety* or *Hollywood Reporter* or any business websites. See which companies are active. Who has an appetite for material with a similar sensibility to your work? A great hunter gets into the mind of its prey. Learn as much as you can about your targets. What movies have they made; what is coming up? Try to see the trailers on the Web.

I would advise *not* attempting to sell a script that is almost a copy of something that has just succeeded for a buyer; rather, try to show buyers a fresh concept that might appeal to their taste. Most creative people don't want to climb the same mountain twice; however, they do adhere to themes and styles in their work. Reading and networking will help you discover and understand these themes. For better information, consider a paid search service like IMDBPro or, if you can afford it, StudioSystem. Both are online data bases that list the current working status of almost every company, studio, and producer, plus all the people in the supplier sides of the business — every writer, director, successful actor, as well as their agents and the projects they have in development, are shooting, and have completed.

Discuss what you have learned from your research with your agents or managers. It will focus your time with them.

BEFRIEND THE ASSISTANTS

Be sincere; show interest in their lives and goals. Networking is an exchange. Many times the assistant is not being treated as a real person, just a functionary. Yet these people know almost as much of the day-to-day world of our industry as their bosses. Many listen in on every phone call the agent or manager makes. Their knowledge is fresh, and if they have read your work and appreciate your ideas, their input can be inspired. They may bring up outlets and prompt their bosses when they see a likely candidate for you.

Assistants are connected to a jungle telegraph of gossip and business information that can help you build your own philosophy. They can be a source for scripts that are selling or are in development across the industry. Reading scripts that are making an impact can deepen your own creative instincts. I highly recommend that you read widely.

Another reason to sincerely befriend your agent's support team? They are frequently agents or managers in training, and without big clients tying them up, they may have the patience and time to become an ally in your creative career. As they grow and succeed, so might you.

I recommend early writers to avoid being signed by a "big" agent with "giant" clients. You are often going to be at the bottom of the deck waiting to get dealt while the kings and queens are getting serviced. Newer agents have more time, and no kings and queens; they can only ascend to the palace court by making *you* succeed. And they have often worked at the desk of the big-timers so they have access to their knowledge and support.

I also have a tremendous preference for agents who are foul-weather friends. Anyone can sell your work when you are hot and you have a hit. Believe me, many of the agents that ignored you on the way up will now be doing incredible mating dances, ruffling their turkey feathers and making many wonderful gobble–gobble sounds of the glory that they will bring you.

Will they give you support when things are not working out? Will they stand by you when the buyer has a conflict, or is bullying? You don't want to be dropped just at the time when things are getting tough. The seducers that suddenly discover you right after a hit are in it to profit from you, not to coach you. Foul-weather friends will be there when it is tough to sell you. They will take the shot on that idea which is unique and out of the mainstream that you love.

CHOOSE REPS WHO HAVE A MORAL COMPASS

I believe that morality in this or any business is a contributor to a long and successful career. A philosopher agent, manager, or lawyer who listens to you, helps you evaluate your thoughts, and guides you to win–win deal strategies will benefit you much more in the long run. And, in the day-to-day exchange of ideas and life issues, this person will be a source of pleasure and humane advice.

Once you have made a sale, the negotiations are usually turned over to the buyer's business affairs team. These people can sometimes be combative and demoralizing. Their job is to make the best deal possible for their side and get you to give up as much as possible. Frequently, there are brinksmanship games like threatening to drop the deal to test your price.

Your reps have seen this all before, can challenge a deal's fairness, and can guide you emotionally to avoid your freaking out! Most industry deals are based on precedents, terms, and prices that are recognized across the business, balanced by your status and the baseline prices and rewards your other works have established. It can take a lot longer than one wants to work through all this, again, a reason to have trust in your representative.

WHAT DO AGENTS WANT IN A WRITER?

Almost no agent will represent anyone off a single script. In order to judge your work and get a sense of your skill and their compatibility, providing two or three scripts is a minimum. Having a few ideas or treatments without any scripts is like a chef waving recipes at restaurant owners and wanting a job without ever having cooked a meal they can taste.

A range of samples of your vision and accomplishments gives the person who may represent you a sense of your creative vision. Agents can judge your compatibility with their own instincts for selling. Hopefully, they will read your material and have a "eureka!" epiphany that your words impassion them, too. (And you know how I feel about passion!)

Agents don't make the majority of their income from selling scripts; they make their money by selling writers to studios to perform writing on already-existing projects. Our representatives love craftspeople (note I didn't say "hacks"), writers who can be sold to studios and producers to work on rewrites. This work is quick to sell and earns good commissions.

A tiny segment of the top writers earns in the hundreds of thousands of dollars a week for this! It is often the bread-and-butter business for an agency.

Writing scripts that end up as samples can seem disheartening, but they will hone your craft. It is a boring axiom: Writers get better by writing. A variety of finished screenplays displays the talent you are selling and will give the agent a fresh "spec" or two — a script unseen by the industry — that can be a door opener and a quick profit for the agent if it were to sell.

It is harder to sell an artistic spec script or to package a director with your dream personal screenplay. Those odds are much longer. Make sure you and anyone who is going to sign you have a similar vision regarding the intent of the relationship.

And if you want to embrace rewriting, most bigger literary agencies know which scripts the studios and producers are trying to bring to fruition. Some keep "Open Writer Assignment Lists" that may be considered confidential. Still, ask your agent or his or her assistant to share the list, or at least discuss the agency's knowledge with you. You might find a writing opportunity that has a special appeal. Remember, it is your job to convince your agent to give you access to these buyers. Pitch them on your vision for a rewrite. This is as much a creative process as any part of the game. You are sharing their reputation now.

When you are in sync with your representatives, they can help you evaluate your ideas, shape them into successful pitches. Strangely, the goal is not to get your scripts sent out, it is to have you get in the *room* with the buyers. Ours is a business of trust, vision, and idea exchanges. Win your agent's confidence and get sent out to *meet* buyers that offer a good chance of paying you to write your vision for the screen (see "Pitching").

BUT I REALLY WANT TO DIRECT!

It is challenging to help a writer grow into a writer-director. Again, this is more reason to choose a foul-weather friend, a philosopher representative. You want someone who shares your goals, will come with you to key meetings, and will lay a foundation so buyers see your work in a context that shows off your potential directing skills.

Are there agents and managers with big hearts out there?

Yes, here are just two examples from the several wonderful people who have supported me as agents. The late Guy

McElwaine, who represented Steven Spielberg for many years, was an amazing story midwife to me. Also, David Wirtschafter represented me for a long time. David worked tirelessly to help me pull together *Moll Flanders*, and get it into production. When the budget was incredibly tight, he waived his fee.

Chapter **10**

YOU AND YOUR STORY GO FOR A RIDE

You are about to have a meeting with potential buyers. This allows you to become the personal commercial for your story in order to get paid to write it. In a way, it is a very familiar social skill, an organized conversation around a specific topic: a story.

PITCHING

Like any good commercial, it's best if it's short and entertaining. Commercials do not list a new car's entire engineering specifications. They show you the potency of the car sweeping autumn leaves high in its wake and young women swooning over the driver.

A PITCH'S JOB IS TO *SELL* YOUR STORY, NOT TO *TELL* IT!

Even finished scripts need to be pitched when you are trying to get them read. All through your career you will be pitching to various prospects, sometimes to producers, directors, even actors. It is a good skill to be able to verbalize your dream quickly, in a passionate and effective way. To a few people, pitching comes naturally. Most quickly acquire a feel for it.

It's okay to be nervous — most people are, a little! You have your meeting; you are going to be the center of attention. I like the extra adrenalin; it makes my memory recall sharper. Although I like wine and celebrations, I have made a habit of not drinking the day before I am going to present something

I consider important. I like to be as sharp as possible. In fact, I like to take up the invitation of a cup of coffee. It makes my mind work a little more quickly. I find that the act of pitching a story can bring new ideas and discoveries as I talk. Pitching tends to grow your story.

I usually have researched the company and, if possible, the persons to whom I am selling. I try to find authentic themes of connection. I have seen their latest movie. The buyer has worked with people I know and like. We both have kids. We both live in the same neighborhood. It is easier to pitch after getting a sense of the humanity of your audience.

In Hollywood, you will mainly be selling to young development executives, people whose role in the company is to work with writers and discover opportunities. These creative executives want to find a movie idea that can get made, as 90% of all scripts do not. Even better, they would like to discover a hit that will get them promoted and grow their careers on the back of a success.

So try to frame your project according to their idea of success. Can you name actors that Hollywood regards as bankable who might be attracted to your leading roles? Using the name and face of a star can conjure a vision of your character in the buyer's head, a financially positive association. Is there a best-selling video game in this? Often, the business has its daily fashions, as movies open and make money. These films become brief pointers to understanding how your concept could break out, too.

What about a science-fiction *Lord of The Rings* or a *Jurassic Park* with killer cavemen getting loose?

The worst pitches we hear are often linear versions of a story from beginning to end, like a train fixed rigidly to the tracks. Frequently, they turn out to be too long and predictable.

The goal is to get your buyers to participate as you go forward. Then you can adapt your concept as the buyers contribute questions and ideas to your vision, thus talking themselves into the project.

Before your meeting, test-drive on friends the simplest, most potent way of verbalizing why this film deserves development. You are sharing your thesis, the best of your Islands of Sanity, your character's nugget, a brief overview of the external story, and your personal style and approach in whichever order feels instinctively appropriate. I have often gotten a deal to develop a project without having every fact in place, but by having enough material to give a powerful sense of what the finished project could be. Pitching is sharing enough of the sizzle so you get paid to cook the meal. Practicing makes the process much less stressful. It gives you guidelines to what is working and what parts to skip over. Remember, the goal is to see your pitch as a conversation with the buyer... a shared event.

In the pitching room, this is your theater. Keep your sense of humor. Grab your audience — give them a shocking or fascinating element of your story to hook them; share your story's discovery. "I had this nightmare that was so scary it stopped me from sleeping; when I told it to my wife, it stopped her too."

Get their curiosity and you have done half the job in your opening sentence.

SUM UP THE PROJECT IN A POSTER LINE

He was a major tennis star... who decided to become a woman! Two eccentric robots and a farm boy take on the mightiest evil in the universe! She killed her brother in a car accident — and now she's coming to her sister's wedding!

I tend to be nonlinear in my pitching, grouping potent thoughts like my character's nugget, the big act breaks, filling in with cool insights and details and personal asides on other films that have influenced this new evolution. I sometimes get quite emotional. I am determined to share my passion for my project. I am never rigid.

Talk about your story in any order that sells it best. Maybe your ending is so powerful it blows people away; then go back and explain how your story will build towards it. Sometimes a pitch will detail the main characters and a couple of amazing things about them before going into more details on the plotting.

We are trying to create a need to know, a desire in the listener to discover the outcome. We are creating curiosity that can only be resolved by hearing out the best elements of the story, or by paying you to find them.

If you want to use notes to help remember points, I recommend index cards so you can quickly flip through them. And then make eye contact and talk to your buyer. I suggest you never plan to read your story. You could just as well have sent a letter and missed the point of a pitch, the human interaction.

When you tell your story, observe the others you are pitching to. Try to judge how much detail to give. Read their body language and pick up on how long to take and what level of detail feels right to emphasize. Too much can blunt their interest and intrude on their day. Be brief. Be authentic. But give them your best stuff in a distilled, energetic, and fun fashion.

Often, the creative executive will take notes on the whole process, which can be disconcerting. Ignore it and play your game; engage and explore your idea with them.

There is a frightening axiom in Hollywood that you can "die of enthusiasm," meaning that people don't want to critique you. They hold back from fear of offending an artist, thus preventing them from other opportunities of working with you. But that reticence is not helpful. Objections conquered put concrete into your foundation.

INVITE QUESTIONS AT THE END

Fish for problems. Books on salesmanship frequently state that once buyers' objections have been overcome they have no reason to resist a sale. Try to find pleasant ways of asking for the things that are preventing a purchase. You might easily have a good answer that can turn things around. Or you may not sell this buyer, but by finding an answer to their objections, you are closer to success with the next one.

SHOW AND TELL?

Whatever helps you strengthen your sale is good. If you feel a piece of memorabilia supports your story (a book, a toy, a powerful photo image, an eyeball in a glass jar!), bring it and let it circulate. We supposedly have many different kinds of emotional intelligences, and buyers can be incredibly varied, from pragmatists to dreamers. Use your gut instincts to do what feels right in order to support your vision.

MEETINGS OFTEN HAVE SURPRISE ENDINGS

It is a good idea to have pre-thought one or two extra story ideas that might be discussed. I have sometimes been asked not to continue a story partway into the process be-cause the buyer already has something like it in development. Instead of wasting the whole meeting, explore your other concepts to get a better idea of the material that these people will buy. I have sold these extra ideas more often than one might imagine.

In one spectacular case, Jeff Sagansky had become head of CBS. Jeff had run Tri-Star Motion Pictures previously, and had greenlighted a movie called *The Kiss*, which I had directed and produced with my Trilogy partners. Now, as the head of a TV network, he invited us to pitch a series idea, if we had one. I went through my lists of concepts, dreamed up some amalgams and some feature ideas that could translate into a series, checked that they worked with John Watson, and we went to pitch Jeff with our TV agent. I started the first pitch, a project called *Space Rangers* about a frontier fort at the edge of the galaxy and the ragged group of ranger heroes defending it. Jeff bought it in the room, a rare thing in TV. He asked if we had any other ideas. I went on to pitch three more concepts that I had prepared just in case the first one failed. Jeff kept buying each one. Being new to TV we had no idea how unusual this was. It was so unusual that our agent stood up on the fourth purchase and said, "That's enough." I am not sure how many more I might have sold if my agent had let me keep going, but all four shows had scripts written, two got made as pilots, and *Space Rangers* was briefly on the air. That day made up for a great many full-blown rejections during a career.

After pitching a story idea, I have frequently been approached by studio executives to rewrite a project that their company is committed to because my new work touches on problems that they are struggling to solve.

SO, BE ADAPTABLE

And what if the meeting feels like a fiasco? You feel like you failed to get to your goals. Here's the deal. You are probably more sensitive and had a lot more at stake than the buyers. They in all probability barely noticed; they may even have *liked you* but failed to buy for any number of reasons.

Oz moves in mysterious ways. Development executives are unlikely to confess that they cannot buy because their budgets have run out or that they are just taking meetings to keep informed. They are unlikely to boast that they have almost no decision power and their bosses didn't buy the idea when they pitched it. Yeah, ugly, but true. Additionally, your efforts may have failed to penetrate a couple of "telephone game" misinterpretations, as the executive shared your story with his or her superiors on the journey to their decision.

Plus — and this is a big plus — in Hollywood, everyone is scared that they will miss out on the next big thing. A great new idea will often get you back in the room!

As a buyer, we often do not judge the story by the quality of the pitch. In fact, we have bought quite badly pitched stories because the story itself was so effective and the writer's other scripts impressed us.

Above all, a pitch is a way for a buyer to get a sense of you, to decide if you might be compatible to work together, and whether your styles mesh. Try to sincerely make the experience positive and engaging. Let your sense of humor free, if it seems right. If you don't sell this idea, your goal is to have left such a good feeling that you are welcomed back to try again.

Chapter 11

HOW DO I SURVIVE UNTIL I GET PAID TO WRITE?

Assuming you don't have an eccentric Uncle Albert who will mortgage his house to pay for your movie, deciding to write screenplays enrolls you in a large and time-honored fellowship, that of the starving artist.

UN-STARVING

Luckily, writing is a relatively inexpensive process. Once you have a basic computer or a pad and paper, you are able to start. But how do you outlast the artistic and gastronomic drought until you break in? I suggest working for a company allied to the business and writing in your spare time.

Seeking work and selling yourself creates anxiety — it can be a tough process. But there are techniques to make it more comfortable. Although a starter job may be lowly, don't think of it that way. You are not looking to become a drone. The instincts that drive your ambition are important things to protect. You are looking for a way to support developing your artistic passions and your business instincts.

If you live in a city that generates major film productions, you should view your job search as a valuable method to study the ecosystem from the inside and make a network of relationships to draw advice and support from as you find time to write. Fellow writers are in this world; their kinship can be a supportive source of collective artistic wisdom and survival techniques. "That executive S.O.B. said that to me too!"

For a large number of reasons, the entertainment industry is not what it appears. Viewed through the prism of movie reviews, TV shows, and the public relations flackery of the studios, it seems like Oz on the hill. The reality is quite different. To sell yourself to business, you must try to find out where the truths lie.

If you are not in a major city with feature businesses, work where creativity happens: an advertising agency, a TV station, or a small video production company. Read biographies of filmmakers you admire, books on writing and breaking in, blogs by industry insiders… with the Internet, it's not so hard to learn the real ecosystem.

JOBS FOR BEGINNERS RANGE FROM:

Production assistants (P.A.s) on productions? Good experience in real filmmaking, but little time to write.

Working in a mail room at a talent agency? A lot of drone and little opportunity to meet creative people or get your hands on scripts.

Working on an agent's desk or as a development executive's assistant? Here you read scripts, as they are being offered to actors and directors, write coverage, make coffee. Jobs, no matter how lowly, don't feel like disposable work when you see your growth path in them.

Writers' assistants? A great one-on-one with a working pro. You may end up picking up the wife's dry cleaning. Or you may be at their side with two keyboards attached to the computer cracking the riddles of the next scene together.

An assistant at a small production company? Here you see the whole development and production process. That includes groups like Trilogy.

HOW DO YOU MEET THOSE IN A POSITION TO GIVE YOU OPPORTUNITIES?

Introductions are helpful from people who know and value you. A letter addressed to your target from a professor or a mentor who really sees something special in you can open doors.

Contacting company executives on the chance they may have a job creates a difficult expectant climate (unless there is a specific role that has been advertised). It puts executives on the spot. Who wants to admit they can't afford to hire anyone, or don't have the power to?

I think it is much less difficult to contact people and ask for career advice. Advice is unthreatening, it is disarming, it shows interest in the person you are meeting.

We call finding solutions to confronting a new and slightly scary goal, like cold-calling a stranger, "framing devices." At Trilogy, we use problem-solving to find framing devices to help get our projects to possible financiers, actors, or directors. Each approach is a challenge. We give each other supportive guidance, suggestions on an opening line, or a sales angle to break that wall of uncertain reticence.

When you are starting out, asking for career advice is a great framing device. It is easy for anyone to talk about their knowledge and how they came up through the ranks. In fact, it can be flattering to be asked. Most people, when they are not crazily busy, like to mentor. Also, many are curious about a new, quality writer and what the younger generation thinks. You may represent the youth audience, a powerful factor in their lives. The great thing about a mentoring conversation: It is an oblique job search, too.

If the conversation goes well, suck up the courage to ask for help. You may be allowed to use their names to generate more opportunities. You could end up with a high-value executive helping to sell you to his or her contacts. It can feel tough to do, but remember: You also have to live with yourself if you don't ask — a 100% error of omission!

Another way to meet those executives and talents in the higher ranks of the business is to have a constructive goal when you want to use their time. Make a video or write an article about them for a valid publication or website, sharing their knowledge so others can benefit from the end result. This gives them a forum and you a purpose for your visit. It enables you to be seen as someone constructive and creates an opportunity for you to learn from their skills and experience while altruistically benefiting others. It's a win/win for all parties.

We will take exploratory meetings at Trilogy, and when we hire, we try to find people with potential. We call it hiring the promotable, people with passion and a sense of direction who want to learn. Confessing your life goals in an interview is a judgment call. It exposes you to seeming like a short-termer. I have no problem hiring someone who wants to write. They are going to understand our goals better. Even if they leave the company, we like to think we have created allies with whom we can network or take pride in their accomplishments.

When you get an interview, illustrate how hard you would work by showing initiative and researching the company or the individual. The more movies of theirs you have seen and can reference, the stronger the opportunity for a bond. In a meeting, we are always impressed when people know our work and have opinions about it. Honest flattery never hurts; fake flattery can seem obsequious. And too much criticism can be a turnoff.

By being honest and enthusiastic at an interview, you enhance your chances of being remembered and brought back when there is an opportunity. We have shared our scripts if we thought it would let us learn more about a prospect and discover how articulate people view our material. Films are both perspiration and inspiration... sometimes a random suggestion from an outsider can evolve into a breakthrough.

YOU CAN'T HOOK A PAYING OPPORTUNITY?

Consider offering to intern for free in companies that really turn you on. Students will pay for academic instruction but see interning for free in the real world as inappropriate after graduating. Try to view learning the real turf as an extension, a graduation semester.

Networking is vital. A lot of websites that group young people working in the industry trade information (called "tracking boards"). Allies on these boards can give you a sense of the ebb and flow of the job openings and spec projects in the ecosystem. It's fun to gossip with friends in the business and watch the currents constantly move as goals change, people shuffle around, management comes and goes, projects fail or succeed.

To survive in Toronto in my early days as a filmmaker I leased a multi-roomed house and rented rooms to young friends who had jobs at various levels in film. We shared food and chores and covered for each other if things got tough. The house was a good place to network with the colleagues of the different house members. It became the birthplace for our company, Insight. The main office was in the downstairs front room with the projector. I slept in the back room, we edited in the basement, and John Watson slept in a cupboard for a while! Shane Black and a similar group of young film guys shared a place they nicknamed the Pad-O-Guys. I think there was some romantic research done there. You will have to press them for details, if they want to reveal them.

As digital technology evolves, it is even becoming possible for the very determined to team up with other creative people, shoot your script with a consumer HD camera, edit on a home computer, and come out with a salable product. Internet distribution systems are breaking the studio stranglehold. The future is fascinating.

Our business manager insists that Trilogy should spend its funds wisely, keep the overhead down, and last as long as possible between opportunities. He's seen people rise and fall, and those that spend like they are up all the time will not last out a dry spell. Good advice: There is no true answer but your own persistence.

If you are going through hell, keep going.
— Winston Churchill

Chapter 12

I MADE A SALE. I'M IN DEVELOPMENT?

**Someone
with money
has embraced
your work.**

TAKE SOME TIME TO CELEBRATE

John Watson is always pointing out that we often forget to luxuriate in a success, however briefly, before we throw ourselves at the next set of problems. It is good for the soul to let those moments of success resonate and feed you, strengthening you for the next step on your journey.

Buyers will ask you to re-craft your vision to support their goals. This can be painful or liberating, depending on how flexible you are and how supportive or knowledgeable your development team is.

Inside the studio and producer ranks, there are great storytellers. And there are also a few rank idiots, folks who think that reading a finished screenplay is the same as having the complete skills to order "improvements." There are no test qualifications for this job. People are hired on the basis of reputation, subjective recommendations, and favoritism. You have to deal with all possibilities. Use your skills, creativity, and patience to work with whatever category you end up with. Outsiders see differently than you do, and will represent a part of your potential audience.

Script changes are inevitable. Your goal is to try to find the value in any insights given to you. Try to discuss your reasoning and listen to theirs fairly. I have managed to craft my way around idiotic suggestions and not damage the purpose of my screenplay. And I have had input that I cherished, which expanded and improved my work immensely. Scripts do grow. They are crafted in layers.

You will often be asked to target your work to the taste of another artist, hopefully a director or an actor who can help move your work forward to the goal of production.

Creative people will have a different voice and this is reasonable. They are adopting your child now and can dress and teach them in their own way. This is going to happen; it comes with working in a communal industry. Remember, when frustrated, it's okay — you chose this business (painting is cheaper and a solo form of art).

If you do have conflicts, try to be patient and work through the process (complain and let off steam to your advisors). Some things are just semantics. You can discover that you are closer than you think — your development executive is just explaining in his or her terms. Build from the things you agree on. Try not to write what is ordered up, but discover the logic in a suggestion. The solution might be to change an earlier scene that steers around a later problem.

The goal for both parties is hope, the possibility of seeing your efforts rewarded with a budget and big screen. Keep going. That can mean many drafts over years... Yeah!

We developed a wonderful script for many years. It went through several studio drafts. The president of the studio signed off. We then got a major Hollywood star interested and we wrote a draft for him. He wanted us to get a certain director onboard, which meant that another vision had to be articulated in another new draft, which then had to be cleared by the studio again. Finally, this was resubmitted to the artist. And on his final reading, he declared he thought he was too old to play the part!

Do you curse your bad luck, or get over it and say, "I had a shot"? You will face as many tests in this game as your heroes do. And that's if you are successful. I have been fired off scripts. I have been obstinate and damaged my relationship with an executive. And I have made changes that others requested that surprised me by how good they became.

But I have had permission to be a paid dreamer. I have overcome many personal fears and obstacles that no other business would have given me. It has been an ongoing, re-markable opportunity to meet fantastic people, in every sense of the word. Major executives have become lifelong friends. John and I have worked with top stars and directors, while coming to understand their needs and goals in the process. As writers and producers, we have helped get many movies made that would never have existed without our efforts.

THREE DEVELOPMENT EXPERIENCES

BLOWN AWAY

Jay Roach and I met with two young writers, John Rice and Joe Batteer, and decided we would encourage them to explore a bomb-squad story set in Boston. Using some of his father's experiences in training anti-terrorist home security forces, Jay outlined a story with Joe and John, who then elected to write it into a spec screenplay. The piece started brilliantly but needed more development time to evolve the second and third acts, and therefore was unlikely to find a sale. John Watson came up with a simple idea to share the first act only with the executives at MGM/UA, without mentioning that anything else had been written. He was able to secure a writing deal for the two writers, who went on to complete the script, which became our production of *Blown Away* with Jeff Bridges, Tommy Lee Jones, and Forest Whitaker.

FLYING TIGERS

John and I developed a project called *Flying Tigers* about young American fighter pilots who volunteered to fly as mercenaries for Claire Chennault in China prior to Pearl Harbor. As writers and producers, we worked on this project for more than fifteen years, setting it up at three different studios, with three different directors — and still it failed to get made. We even had WWII jungle airfield sets and airplanes built, as it was so close to being filmed, but to no avail. We heard that it had accumulated more than ten million dollars of development costs. We still believe that somebody will make a great flying tigers movie and, hey, ours is still available!

HOUDINI

John Watson and I made a documentary on magicians in America, which included a section on Harry Houdini, including filming his annual Halloween séance. The experience stayed with me and caused me to conjure a plot, not for a movie but for a Broadway-style musical that took place on a vaudeville theater stage that had been transformed into a radio broadcasting studio in 1936, where the tenth and final anniversary séance was to take place, with Houdini's wife present.

During the séance, Houdini himself was to return as a spirit and realize that, while he wanted to show the world that he could escape from death, he had discovered even more; he wanted to tell his wife, whom he'd let down and underappreciated during his life, just how much he loved her.

I tried for two years to find a writer who was experienced in musicals to write this plot that impassioned me. They all said I should write it myself. Finally, in a three-week frenzy, I wrote the entire book and lyrics. To my surprise, Sam Cohen, a major Hollywood and Broadway agent, responded strongly to it and tried for a while to set it up, but ultimately to no avail. Rather than give up on the project, I chose to rewrite it into a non-musical movie screenplay, keeping the same séance plot and love story, all while I was doing press tours in twelve different cities premiering *Moll Flanders*.

Upon my return, I showed the script to my agent, David Wirtschafter, who said, "It's terrible. Don't show it to anybody!" I was a bit shell-shocked, but... I went back to work on it anyway, and created a much more refined draft.

John suggested that I show the script to TNT which was making award-winning feature movies for its network. Julie Weitz, the head of original programming, said she would buy the project, subject to discussing an issue with the script. I expected that she would want to chop up and change my script for TV. Julie said one specific thing to me: "Could we see more of Bess Houdini in the montage sequences?" That was it — and she was right, too. With that one change, we made a deal, and I directed the movie for TNT starring Johnathon Schaech, Mark Ruffalo, Paul Sorvino, Rhea Perlman, Ron Perlman, Stacy Edwards, and a young Emile Hirsch.

Development is unpredictable.

Chapter 13

BEATING
THE BLUES

Each of us reacts to our life paths in different ways. I have friends who seem totally oblivious to stress. Lucky devils. On the other hand, I've felt stress almost my whole adult life, especially when I am putting myself up for a challenge, taking a new creative path, meeting new people, calling a potential buyer to hype my projects. And sometimes I seem to experience anxiety just because I do!

A FILMMAKER'S "POSITIVE" THOUGHTS ON STRESS

I'd be lying to say that stress doesn't color my approach to my work.

In my early twenties I hit a stress wall, punching up a high score on those psychological charts that count "stressors." *Did you move homes? Have you changed jobs? Have you taken on a new relationship?* And so on. Even a *vacation* can be a stressor. No kidding.

Back then, I'd quit working for a salary, taking on landlord responsibilities and sharing the house with a flock of itinerant filmmakers. My wife-to-be, Wendy, moved in with me, and I started a film company with John Watson, with no cash resources, just ambition.

I ran my emotional batteries flat trying to keep all these plates spinning: tight chest, gritting jaw, panicky feelings. I felt a frequent sense of being out of control and dark forces coming at me, all without any real, hard-core issues to deal with. My anxiety seemed to revolve around things that "might" happen: my own possible failure, disasters and rejections that I imagined, zero proven realities, but they sure felt real to my body.

I decided to try to study why I felt so freaked-out. I read books that claimed they could help me cope. What I found was rather staggering: Stress is normal. It's biologically built in to help us!

Stress is evolution's attempt to give us predictive vision. What will happen if I go into that cave? Should we eat this fruit? Should I challenge that alpha male? Stress is our imagination harnessed to try to outguess the future. It probes with an unconscious feedback loop. Our mind's eye sees a multiplicity of possible outcomes. We often feel them, too! Butterflies in the stomach, the flight-or-fight response… our imagination sets off our internal chemistry to ready us for action.

I've read studies that claim that the smarter you are the more stress you feel. Who would have thought that we artists, with big imaginations, could happily be feeding ourselves an endless cycle of frightening what-ifs and sweaty-palm maybes? As a survival mechanism, primitive fighting-or-flighting does not seem to be a useful addition to your story-pitch meeting. Or does it?

I also realized that the adrenalin produced by my anticipation of a challenge, like a pitch meeting, was actually helpful. That extra zing was like human-produced caffeine. It made me alert. It provoked me to think faster and to read the emotions of others. It made my memory better and stimulated new effective ideas in the room. I've learned to rely on my adrenalin to give me an edge.

Come on. How can feeling nervous be good?

Look at the bright side. We are survivors bred from millions of generations of ancestors whose nervous thinking prevented them from any major blunders before they could mate. Inherently, we are the descendants of winners, winners with great imaginations and, in some cases, very fast feet (uneaten winners)!

But why does it have to feel so uncomfortable?

From my research, something very unusual came to light; we actually get to choose how we feel under the effect of stress. We can make it feel good.

Huh? Being robbed at gunpoint or being the victim of a surprise birthday party gives your body an identical flight-or-fight physiological reaction. But we perceive that reaction in two different ways.

> *Adopting the right attitude can convert a negative stress into a positive one.*
> — Dr. Hans Selye, stress expert

Anxiety can become *excitement* if you value why you are experiencing the feeling. A roller-coaster ride is scary, but we love it!

If you can see your *adversities* as *adventures*, they become more enjoyable. Palpitations, sweat, excess nervous energy… we love stress when cheering on our favorite team in the play-offs. In fact, we would feel cheated if we were remote and calm while the whole season comes down to a few seconds!

Hans Selye, the late Canadian stress expert, asks us to try to see our stress as "eustress" (coined from the "eu" in euphoria), instead of "distress." Accepting your stress, viewing it as the cost of aiming for a positive goal, changes the way you interpret your own inner chemistry.

In fact, directing a feature film for me is the most grueling, demanding, and scary process. But I see it as an adventure even though some days it is raw exhausting pain to get out of bed. But I can't wait to do it again.

This changing of your perceptions can even apply when you are experiencing deeply dark challenges if you can find something in the experience that fits your value system.

The innovative psychologist Viktor Frankl wrote a book, *Man's Search for Meaning*, in which he describes being imprisoned in a concentration camp in World War II. He tried to find a positive in his captivity by studying the process. He discovered that the strong captives could die by just giving up if they lost their reason for living. And weak people could go on with the spirit of a lion if they retained a purpose, such as the will to stay alive for the sake of their children.

> *Everything can be taken from a man but... the last of the human freedoms — to choose one's attitude in any given set of circumstances, to choose one's own way.*
>
> — Viktor Frankl

Victor evolved his discovery that perceiving a purpose in adversity can harness a healthier attitude and better coping skills. He termed this process "logotherapy" and used it as a treatment to help others.

> *What man actually needs is not a tensionless state but rather the striving and struggling for some goal worthy of him. What he needs is not the discharge of tension at any cost, but the call of a potential meaning waiting to be fulfilled by him.*
>
> — Viktor Frankl

Both Frankl and Selye independently pointed to one, powerful emotional coping mechanism, that is, to bear the stress because you are doing something you value. They both were convinced that life's toughest challenges were far more comfortable if you could see a positive, even spiritual, goodness in your goals.

They didn't mean that you had to become a saint. Frankly, earning money to feed your children makes that work valuable. And if you have a philanthropic goal for some of that money, too, great. But the concept that Selye called "Altruistic Egoism" was simple. If you value facing a burden to help others, the burden will seem less dark and defeating. In fact, it might transform into an ego-gratifying experience.

Let's say you believe that the movie you want to produce is socially important. Your "passion" (remember that word?) gives you power. You will find yourself able to fight longer and stronger. And remember, only you judge what is socially important, or whatever purpose, belief, commitment, or reward that brings out your passion is right for you. Compare that feeling with trying to get a movie made that does not impassion your values. One project will feel like a mission and the other a chore.

The stress I felt in my twenties never came back as potently. I think it had to do with the time in life when I had not yet tested myself and carried many hopes, ambitions (and a delusion or two thrown in for good measure). We may be immensely creative, courageous, and industrious, but the world doesn't know it yet. Entering the adult world means making adjustments.

A few people will become the next Steven Spielberg at twenty-five, but others may have to take a more conventional route and should not criticize themselves if they have to take a starter job that includes making coffee and mail runs. It's sort of like thinking we should be a billionaire at twenty-five and then berating ourselves for failing! I call this phase of life "your dreams hitting your realities."

It can feel demoralizing, starting out. But the great thing about this period is that once you navigate it, everything you do is built on the foundations of your real skills, your real nature. This is concrete, compared to untested ambitions. From this point on your life lessons add up; you are building a solid personal structure. Sure you have some frustrations, failures, and doubts. But your inner artistic voice is being trained as these tests develop your problem-solving strengths.

Starting any career can be full of emotional zaps that surprise like jack-in-the-boxes. The trap can open at any time, and something scary can happen. But the next time the same trap opens and jack jerks up, the effect is far less potent. It's called "de-conditioning." When you've seen the same problem enough times it wears out its power to scare you.

But what if I fear that I'm going to lose control and freak out?

There are an unlucky few of us who can experience really panicky thoughts. These mental forms have been called "Imaginary Bears." We do such a great job of dreaming up an unpleasant outcome (that hasn't happened) that we can create a wondrous stress monster. Our Imaginary Bear can be such a scary creation that it triggers our internal chemistry.

We literally panic ourselves with ideas: What if I lose my job? Get rejected by someone I value? What if the story I pitch is going to get me laughed out of the room? What if I just freak out?

Because we trigger our chemistry, we tightly associate a thought with a real chemical outcome. We literally invent a Bear, and it can be so ugly we don't want to think about it. We try to mentally push away the mind's vision of that horrible outcome. We try to escape our Imaginary Bear. And damn it — in the process we are conditioning our body to react to defend us! The more the thing freaks us out, the more our body pours on the chemistry. Adrenalin, pounding heart, mind flipping around generating dozens of escape thoughts, gasping breath — we can experience a full stress menu as our body tries to fight and flight away from itself. We call this nasty nerve cycle a panic attack.

If we encountered a real obstacle, our mind would flow into problem-solving mode. It would become occupied, get to grips planning and strategizing (which it is really good at). But with the Imaginary Bear, you keep thinking, "What if this thing gets out of my mind cave and freaking eats me?"

So what's the cure?

It doesn't have to be that way. Slow down. Be kind to yourself. Stop being critical of yourself and indulge in some personal forgiveness. Find the right time and place, somewhere comfortable, where you can do some undisturbed thinking. You are going to do the one thing that will catch the Imaginary Bear at its own game. You are going to de-condition your fear loop and imagine it attacking you.

When you invite in the ideas that frighten you, two things happen: (1) You are choosing and controlling the battle; and (2) You are teaching your body not to react. No matter how awful, ugly, embarrassing, and foul that Bear idea is, it is imaginary. And believe me, our minds are capable of evolving some thoughts that make some juicy, darn repugnant, antisocial, and horrifying Bears. But, when you focus and use your mental resources to embrace that Bear, pulling into yourself all its contaminating ideas and horrible consequences, it soon starts to become obvious that the Bear isn't real. No real bear, no real risk from which to run away. The Imaginary Bear evaporates by being invited in as you are creating a non-flight-or-fight reaction to your fear. Dorothy, your witch is melting!

Inviting Bears to attack you with all the color and imagination you have wears away at the conditioning. You bring that Imaginary Bear out of its cave. No power, no fangs: A pompously powerful creature can become ridiculous in the light of being embraced.

Keep doing this, accepting and reveling in the thoughts that scared you. What if you did run out of the room, did get rejected by your boss, did run down the street naked? Killing Bears with kindness can be quiet fun. Many are the time I have finally thought, "What the hell have I been worrying about that for?"

TELL ME SOME MORE GOOD THINGS ABOUT STRESS

Stress makes you more empathetic to others. Admit to it; share it. A stiff upper lip might work on a battlefield, but in the arts sometimes it is healthier to wear your heart on your sleeve and discover kindred spirits.

Stress can give you the gift of insight. It can make you more poetic, more aware of the human condition; it is a dark gift, but a gift nevertheless. Some of the greatest men, from Churchill to Lincoln, struggled with their regular, darker moments. Churchill called it his "Black Dog." But they did not get disabled by their depressive times. They learned coping skills to dig themselves out or learned to watch and mitigate their symptoms. It is recorded that Lincoln, during the darkest days of the Civil War, read humor books at his cabinet meetings. He read until everyone was laughing so much tears ran. Then, when they had changed their mood, they got down to business. Both men were creative, as well as pretty damn good writers.

Success is the ability to go from one failure to another with no loss of enthusiasm.
— Winston Churchill

Life can be shockingly tough. Sometimes we take a real blow. Fate sneaks up and steals something from us. Remember, though, what you feel today is not a permanent state of mind. Time will change things. This is just some stormy weather, so put up your mental umbrella. And if you are feeling a little out of balance, there is no shame whatsoever in seeking a counselor to help organize your thoughts or help balance your chemistry. Do what feels right to you. Don't let others tell you to buck up out of it. Find your own time table and navigate on intuition and feelings until your strengths return. They mostly do return, maybe not the same as before, but shaped by the experience. We humans are resilient, creative, and problem-solving. Time heals, humor heals, love heals.

That's how I see it. How am I with my stress? Brilliant some days, a little blue others, like everyone. But better than I used to be, thanks.

STRESS-REDUCING ACTIONS

Accept that there is no off switch for stress in our body. But you can live with it, wear it down, mold it, take charge of it. Use it.

Decide to be yourself. Be authentic; don't try to be who you are not. Each time you present the real you, your personality, confidence, and drives get stronger. The real you is always there and can be relied on.

Be human. Don't fear mistakes. Being perfect is impossible. Let out your sense of humor, laugh at your foibles, don't be so serious.

Don't be overprotective of your ideas. Don't let worrying about being cheated stop you from sharing your creativity. Out of my whole career I can only think of one or two instances where my efforts were purloined or I was damaged. And, after a brief spell of anger, I decided the best outcome was to pity the jackass and move on rather than waste my time going backwards to take revenge. I know I will have more ideas!

Take the time to pre-visualize. Just like before you fall asleep, train your mind to imagine a positive path. This works in sports and it works in life. Envision your goals as vividly as you can mentally draw them. I like to think of myself with an

Oscar in my hand. Rehearse pitches and important situations with friends and co-conspirators.

Believe passionately in what you sell. Remember, you chose this career. There is a salesman's axiom that you should believe enough in your product that you are sorry for those that don't buy it.

When you are ready, invite and look forward to critiques and discussion about your project. Every obstacle raised is a chance for you to eliminate an objection to the sale. Each time you find a solution, the buyer — be it an actor, director, financier — gets more deeply committed. You are joining them to your project by overcoming their doubts.

Be prepared for rejections. We chose a competitive business. Many people out there are trying to get to the same budgets and opportunities. Expect it to take time. Look at your job as collecting rejections and collect as many as you can. Have as many projects out there that you believe in, because it increases your odds. In his book, a study of randomness and statistical distribution called *The Drunkard's Walk,* Leonard Mlodinow states that a bad product and a good product have an equal statistical random chance of succeeding. We are not good judges of success — look at lottery players! Randomness plays a giant factor in our lives, outside of our ability to observe or measure. In other words, getting your work exposed could be the most vital thing you do so that luck can help you. On my *Houdini* script I kept a wall chart to see if I could get to one thousand rejections! It was a coping strategy to make the hundred or so I did get, before the movie sold, seem less important. But it kept me exposing my material to the God of Randomness.

We tend to think that others are traveling an easier, straight line, and we are the ones with the tough road. NOT TRUE! They are probably hitting as many bumps as you are, just not the same ones and not at the same time, and not necessarily publicly.

Some of your buyers may be more stressed than you are. One studio head we knew, a great guy, was famous for barely speaking in meetings. A long meeting could pass with him having only uttered a word or two. It would really throw us. But he seemed to cope with his immense shyness. His staff would fill in the gaps, and he was a tremendously successful film executive for many years.

We all live our lives in our bodies like captains of sailing ships, constantly tacking and tucking to reach our goals. Emotional weather changes or mood currents can lead us astray... this is *normal*. Frequently we have no idea why our brain feels cloudy and rainy or why some days the sun comes out in our head. Don't berate yourself for feeling blue occasionally. And when you feel on top of things, use the good times to make your hard calls.

When emotions seem overwhelming, talk to someone caring. I had trouble admitting my problems. I was embarrassed to intrude on others. But I found that really caring people value your trust. Verbalizing your nervous feelings crystallizes your swirling stress-mess into clearer mental images. It helps you pick apart the reasons for your mood and accelerate your process of working through it.

I don't mean to be a nag, but avoid excessive drugs or drinking. Exercise drains excess adrenalin from your body. Try to sleep regularly; it is amazingly recuperative. Give yourself permission to take naps, too. And take breaks or vacations, a time-out for yourself to recharge. Frequently, I come back from a break to discover that my problem-solving skills seem turbo-charged. I realize on my return — by observing the ease with which powerful, solution-finding measures come to me on a fresh start — how burned-out I was before the break.

Don't defeat yourself. There is a painful little behavior called "The Imposter Syndrome." I have struggled so much to make a project coherent and successful that it made me question my abilities. I felt guilty when others praised the work. I have also experienced the opposite, when something came so easily, I felt guilty for charging for it! We are strange creatures.

As I have noted, my biggest defeats have come when I failed to go forward with something out of doubt. My failed attempts at pursuing my goals have never bugged me as much as the ones I never undertook. They guaranteed me 100% failure. Better to be a little scared now, rather than live a life of regret. If your project impassions you, there must be someone out there who will feel the same way.

Treat yourself like your own best friend would. Encourage yourself, have a healthy ego about when you have been praised, what you have succeeded with. Take the time to remember and visualize when you have been winning. That doesn't mean be obnoxious; it means be confident.

Let me give you one example of how you never know how close you are to success. When John and I started Insight Productions in Toronto, we asked nine children each to use our company to write and direct one-minute commercials selling "life" as if it were a commercial product. It was our mission to prove how imaginative and visually literate children were, a kick back at the educational film companies that we each worked for, which created dispiriting, uninspiring films, purely for profit.

Our kids, ranging in age from eleven to fifteen, made commercials in which chess pieces bickered mightily about their positions on the board, until they were put in the box; in which a manic car salesman sold a military tank and the slaughter it could bring; in which a couple in their eighties just showed their love for each other. Even John Watson was roped in to be the actor who plunged out of a giant peanut to the slogan: "Don't be a nut. Break out of your shell and live!" We called the final short film that combined all the commercials *Life Times Nine*, a joyous anthology of optimism, humor, and touching emotions.

And… WE COULDN'T GIVE THE MOVIE AWAY. We held a big premiere; no press came. The kids were disappointed. One of them said to me, "Why not get us an Oscar?" I just laughed.

But that night — literally in my bathtub — I thought, what a nitwit I was! The film and the kids' work was breakout. It deserved to be seen. I should at least find out what it took to enter a short film for an Academy Award. The following day, I called the Academy from Toronto, feeling like I was intruding on the Vatican of the film world, and was informed that only films that played in a paying theater in Los Angeles for a week were eligible. I had no idea how to accomplish this.

But I decided to phone the manager of an independent Toronto movie theater for advice. His response, in colorfully vulgar language, was to forget it. The whole thing would be too much trouble for any Hollywood theater, especially for a bunch of unknowns from Canada.

I almost quit there, feeling I was on a self-made fool's errand.

But I hung in for one more call to Mitch Woolrich, the man who sold our films to schools in Canada. I knew he represented a couple of California-based short films.

He was sorry, but knew his contacts never dealt with theatrical situations. Mitch said the only living person he knew in Los Angeles was an old buddy whose dad ran a limousine-rental service. We were about to give up, when he said, "Ah, what the heck."

Five minutes later, Mitch called back, "You are in L.A. You have a movie theater!"

Amazingly, the limo service's offices were right next door to a theater (today, the WGA's screening facility). The limo guys took in the movie theater's deliveries all day before it opened. Screening our short was its way to return the goodwill.

Life Times Nine ran for its week. It was one of three live-action shorts nominated for an Oscar that year. And with the help of many caring people, we were able to fly all nine children to the Awards ceremony, a trip of a lifetime. We didn't win an Oscar, but the film was now accepted; it won more than a dozen awards around the world and put our company, and the visual creativity of our young people, firmly on the map.

The *Life Times Nine* experience taught me to keep going no matter how foolish I felt. All through my career, I have taken chances and fought for the things I've believed in and have seen myself occasionally, surprisingly rewarded by the Gods of Randomness. Keep trying. Great things can happen.

Chapter 14

THOUGHTS FROM OTHER SCREENWRITERS

Writing can often be fairly isolating. But when I do spend time with other writers, over lunch with Shane Black at Hollywood's Musso and Frank Grill, or sharing a barbecue with Laeta Kalogridis and her family, I'm always reminded that no two writers think about our process identically. Rather than being the only voice in this book, I approached other successful screenwriter friends and colleagues, and posed this open-ended invitation:

I would love for you to write something intuitive that you would value sharing with newer writers: the way you solved a creative problem, overcame doubt, a technique that has made the process easier — even a sentence which just says, "Write - Write - Write!"

I'm proud and grateful to share these results of my inquiry. I am sure you will find them to be honest, funny, insightful, and encouraging.

Lethal Weapon,
The Monster Squad,
The Last Boy Scout,
Last Action Hero,
The Long Kiss
Goodnight,
Kiss Kiss
Bang Bang
(writer/
director)

SHANE BLACK

To me, fear is summed up in a convenient little mantra: *I'm not going to get the things I want, and I'm gonna lose the things I have already.* And the idea of getting your hopes up? What are you, nuts? What if they get slapped down again? Better to expect the worst, right?

I actually used to think that way. But somewhere along the way, I heard a story I found useful: My agent David Greenblatt shared it with me; it's called "The Jack Story."

The Jack Story's about a guy who's driving and, boom, his tire blows out in a rainstorm. By the side of the road, flat. He sees a farmhouse in the distance with a light on, and he thinks, I don't have a jack, I can't change a tire — but maybe the farmer has one. So he starts walking through the rain and the mud and he thinks, "Well, wait a minute, what if I get to the farmhouse and the guy doesn't have a jack? Then I gotta walk all the way back and I'm getting rained on and it's murder." He starts to panic.

AT WHICH POINT: He takes a soggy breath, says, "Easy, guy. Calm down, it hasn't happened yet, see what happens, play it by ear, okay?"

So he keeps walking and he thinks, "Hmm, what if the farmer HAS a jack, I get all happy — but I bring it back and it's the *wrong kind*. Then I've made this whole trip, and I gotta walk back, WITH the jack !"

AT WHICH POINT: He bites back a sob — Relax. It hasn't happened, just relax...

Three-quarters of the way there, he thinks: "What if the farmer has a jack, it's even the right kind, but suppose he just doesn't want to give it to me, and he says, "I don't know you, f##k you, go out in the rain!"

So the point of the story is, by the time he gets to the farmhouse, he knocks and the farmer comes to the door, "Hello?" and our guy says, "*You know what, buddy, you can take your jack and shove it up your a##!*"

You get the idea. Every so often, I have to remind myself to not make decisions based on imaginary conversations. It's just wasted fear time, spent on all the bad things that could happen, instead of the really interesting things that might.

You might not sell a script. You might not be good. You might this and you might that. What's the point in going down that path? There is none. I know it's tough to say, "Don't be afraid," or "Think positive," but... there really is just no other way to go. You're up against a wall, you've decided you want to do something, you're having some adversity — you can either play out your hand or quit. And I suggest that... My career came down to one moment like that.

I was working on a script called *Shadow Company* in 1984, and I was on page 1, and I showed it to someone — he hated it. I slumped in my chair and I thought, "I can't do this. I sat down to write a screenplay — What was I thinking? I'm a loser." And I nearly gave up. For good, right there.

I'm a one-finger typist. I said — "Just do it." *I held my typing forefinger in the air.* In retrospect, I believe everything came down to that index finger.

Because it descended and hit a key. I just DID it. It took such an effort. I wanted to be anywhere else, doing anyTHING else.

I typed: *The... rain... lashes... the... ground...* I hit keys — Grumbling. Cursing. Mouthing, I hate this, I f##king hate this — until suddenly I was NOT saying that. I stopped, squinted at the page — and glory be, that's a good line. What would our guy say in response? Okay, I'll try this on for size, hmmmm... And three pages later, I had a scene, and it became a script — and it was seen, and read — and it got me *Lethal Weapon*.

It's all about TAKING ACTION. And keeping on with it, mechanically, if need be — until something becomes, even briefly, more interesting to you than your own fear. Until you get caught by the words.

It came down to this. I had a piece of paper in a typewriter and my finger poised to hit one key and I couldn't do it. All I wanted to do was stop. And I hit the key. And now I have a career. So that's the leap of faith.

I walked through that particular fear. You can walk through anything. That's the fabulous truth that I've discovered, that fear never goes away. But it doesn't stop you from putting one foot in front of the other.

*My Big Fat Greek
Wedding
(Oscar Nominee,
Best Original
Screenplay),
Connie and Carla,
I Hate
Valentine's Day,
Larry Crowne*

NIA VARDALOS

I guess it's strange, but I don't consider myself a female writer. I don't adhere to or respect categories, social restrictions, gender, and age limitations. Fortunately, I am immature and naive: both good qualities for survival in this cesspool of an industry. You have to have the optimism of a Vegas gambler to work in Hollywood. I worked very hard on my first screenplay, and didn't pay much attention to the stories of how difficult it would be for an unknown first-time writer to sell a script. And then I got incredibly lucky.

Since the success of *My Big Fat Greek Wedding*, I can tell when I walk into a room whether I am encountering someone who sees my career as the epitome of what is possible, or as a fluke. I have been met with elation, resentment, joy, and anger. I understand what I represent: I am embraced by optimists and an easy target for the disenchanted.

It doesn't matter. I keep writing. And when it's not there, I walk away from my computer. You can't force creativity. I do sit down to write every day. I don't implode when I have a scene that's not working. Yes,

I obsess when I can't figure out the clearest way to express a thought on paper, but I don't get scared. I have learned the best thing to do is walk away. I press Save and go do something else: have coffee with girlfriends, play with my daughter, walk my dog... and somehow, in time, like a chess move, the scene unravels itself in my head, and I sit back down to write. Every day, if ideas are flowing, I write. If not, I go shopping. I have two mottos I live by: Any decision made in fear is a reaction rather than an action. And you're never too fat for a new purse.

I believe that as someone is writing, alone in a drafty office, day after day... if you don't have a voice in your head telling you you're a fraud and no one will ever buy this script, then you're probably not very good. If you love your first draft, it probably sucks. Writers are supposed to keep learning, continue to grow, reach, strive for the best line, the better scene, the perfect way to describe an emotion. That said, I have an awesomely perfect first draft of a screenplay; anyone wanna buy it?

DANNY MCBRIDE

When I took my first step into drafting an actual script, I, like most would-be writers, ran out and purchased a stack of expensive screenwriting books. Though many were very informative in regards to story, scenes, arcs, and characters, the strict formatting sections were often confusing as they varied from author to author. After struggling through several books, I finally began borrowing actual produced scripts. Then it hit me: Most scripts are different, and not just stylistically or story-wise, but *formatting-wise*, and it became quite clear that the formatting rules were really just a collection of guidelines.

One resource I began to value was Drew's-Script-O-Rama. The site had a few hundred scripts available (for free!), and I was shocked when I began to read through different drafts of the same film. It was eye-opening to discover how much things could change during development. *American Beauty*, for instance, as originally envisioned by Alan

Ball, began its early stages as a courtroom drama. Little discoveries like that one helped me to prepare for development in the real world. Soon I began to devour as many award-winning scripts as I could get my hands on. This was an enormous help and a noteworthy exercise that I still practice to this day. Sure, you can sit down and watch a slew of DVDs before you begin your next project — and I often still do! — but I personally don't think there is anything more informative or rewarding than reading a fantastic script.

World Trade
Center

ANDREA BERLOFF

Here we are at the beginning: 120 (or less!) blank pages stare us in the face. It's exciting. Think of the possibilities! And yet... And yet it's also scary as hell. I've written script after script after script and every time, day one, it's terrifying. How are all these strands of ideas, characters, jokes, plot lines, tragic denouements, and spectacular action sequences going to coalesce into one integrated, kick-ass screenplay? The honest answer: Sometimes they don't.

But, then again, sometimes they do.

And it's the sometimes-they-do that keeps me going, compels me to isolate myself from family and the Internet and all semblance of a social life. Because nothing feels better than the sometimes-they-do. And if you have the ambition to take on this monumental task, then something inside you must have once upon a time achieved a little slice of that sometimes-they-do. You know what you can achieve when it's just the blank paper and your brain and a sprinkling of magic that makes the whole thing come together. And you know how good it feels.

Maybe the final screenplay will be messy. But, then again, maybe — just maybe — it won't be. Either way, the journey will be a thrill.

The Curious Case of Benjamin Button (Oscar Nominee, Best Adapted Screenplay), Lucky You, The Good Shepherd, Munich (Oscar Nominee, Best Adapted Screenplay), Ali, The Insider, The Horse Whisperer, The Postman, Forrest Gump (Oscar Winner, Best Adapted Screenplay), Mr. Jones, Memories of Me, Suspect, The Nickel Ride, The Concorde... Airport '79

ERIC ROTH

I think what makes me at peace while writing is that it is the only time I am completely alone. I realized recently that I spent my life sharing a room. From the time my brother lay across the room from me, through a college roommate, becoming married at eighteen, and finding love again twenty-five years later, I have always shared a room. All the sights and sounds, the pairings and grapplings, the discussions, even when in the throes of sleep, were always for me in tandem. The sweet silence of just whatever comes out of my fingers, what is singularly my own, being alone is a grand joy. Every day for forty-odd years I have relished that solitude to take an adventure into a space I have never traveled and back again on just the seat of my pants. Even the times when the journey between one word and the next was as painful as a cracked heart, when fear of what comes next would rise up and make the next word seem like the largest chasm, those are just and welcome. This is what I can tell you. I am blessed by something more than myself that lets me rummage around my head and pour it out for good or for ill. Call it God, or Mozart, or the middle eye, I get to walk down the hall, close the door, and disappear.

Robin Hood:
Prince of Thieves
(co-writer),
A Gnome
Named Gnorm
(co-writer),
The Zoo Gang,
The Magnificent
Seven (TV),
Breaking News
(TV),
Taking Liberty
(TV pilot)

JOHN WATSON

I have recently discovered the joy of adapting some of my favorite novels to screenplay. It's a pleasure, because I so much enjoy delving deeper into books I love, and trying to figure out what are the essential elements that made the underlying material so appealing to me in the first place. Inevitably there is a massive amount of shrinkage that needs to happen, and ultimately also a fair amount of invention or reinvention, but the key is how to convey the essence of the original and recreate for a movie audience the core emotions you experienced when first reading it.

It starts with endings — where do you want to end up? How do you want the audience to feel when the lights go up? It is sometimes the same place as the novel, but not necessarily. Next, the beginning — the same applies. Then I go through the book and identify the must-have moments, what I like to call (thanks to Pen Densham), "Islands of Sanity." These are the critical events and story beats which propel the narrative. They tend to coincide with Act Breaks, the story's major turning points. If I am appropriately tough on this process, I end up with no more than five truly essential beats, the islands. Then to progress from island to island, to take the narrative through the necessary steps to connect the islands, you need "stepping stones."

The islands are almost always derived from the novel, and the stones usually so, but as I move forward to outline from there, I find I am constantly needing to condense, delete plot points, combine characters, and so forth, in order to squeeze the remaining story and character needs into the screenplay form. By this process I find that I end up with basically the same number of major scenes that I would have in an original screenplay.

My first drafts tend to be very faithful to the original, but I usually discover that further reinvention is required as I move on to later drafts and respond to input from other readers. After the first draft, the priority has shifted, but only slightly, from a respectful recreation of a novel into a script for a film that must of necessity stand alone.

*The Jane Austin
Book Club
(writer/director),
Memoirs of a
Geisha,
Practical Magic,
Matilda,
The Perez
Family,
Little Women,
Shag,
Cuba Crossing*

ROBIN SWICORD

When I sold my first screenplay in 1980, I didn't know a simple statistic that might have made me hesitate before going head-long into writing movies: Out of thousands of working screenwriters, only a handful were women. What I didn't know couldn't stop me. I wrote a movie that I wanted to see, and I found an agent willing to try and sell it for me. The screenplay was a comedy, "Stock Cars For Christ." MGM bought it. It was never made. After writing and selling screenplays fairly steadily for five years, I still had no screen credit. I began enviously to peruse the end-of-year Writers Guild Award ballots, which go out to WGA members for us to elect a "best original" and "best adapted" screenplay. Here on the ballot were all of the English-language movies that year, and under each title, the names of all the lucky writers who had seen their work produced. I wasn't on the lookout for anything in particular as I glanced over the ballot; I was just feeding my envy. But something odd struck me, a small thing that suddenly seemed glaringly obvious: Only three women's names were listed anywhere among the writers on the ballot. Three lone names, among hundreds of male writers who had gotten a screen credit that year. I noted that two of the women were paired with male writing partners.

Curious, I called the WGA's membership office and requested ballots from previous years. As I looked over the previous decade's ballots, I saw what I had not known when I set out to become a screenwriter: Women didn't write the movies that were getting made.

I began to pressure the Writers Guild to make a study: Was there discrimination? At what stage was it happening? Among agents refusing to take female writing clients? At the story department level in the studios? Did an unconscious bias exist among producers when they hired writers? Was bias an unconscious factor in determining which movies were greenlighted? After nearly twenty years of hearing from me, the WGA finally commissioned a study on employment access, which confirmed what women writers in the Guild already knew from their own lives, and verified what Dr. Martha Lauzen at the Center for the Study of Women in Television and Film had been reporting for over a decade: There's a seemingly impenetrable Celluloid Ceiling for women who work in most aspects of film. How permeable is that ceiling? Dr. Lauzen's 2009 report shows that women comprised 16% of all directors, executive producers, producers, writers, cinematographers, and editors working on the top 250 films the previous year.

Would it have been better to know all of this before I dedicated myself to becoming a filmmaker? Or is it better not to be aware of the obstacles we face? I found myself having to constantly weigh similar thoughts when I became a parent of two daughters. How do I help my two intelligent, creative daughters be strong and mentally free in the face of subtle bias? How do I prepare them to thrive in a world or a career where they might not be fully valued?

Anyone who has ever overcome a seemingly impossible obstacle knows the simple answer that silences these
questions: Do it anyway.

Write your script anyway. Direct your movie. Is there a
barrier? Go around it. Ignore conventional wisdom if it doesn't
serve your goal. Use your own judgment. Break the rules, if
the rules don't make sense for you. When you succeed, no
one will mind that you didn't do things "their way." When
you fail, accept the blame. Apologize and begin again. Keep
going. I don't believe that ignorance is always bliss: I like to
know what I am up against, so that I can ignore it. Make
alliances, if you can. There's strength in a common goal.
Whatever is impeding you eventually becomes irrelevant
when you follow your intention, and do good work.

Not sure that you know how to do good work? Do it
anyway.

White Squall,
Lonely Hearts
(writer/director)

TODD ROBINSON

1. There's one common thing that connects all successful people: They never quit. Just because you do not quit does not ensure success, but quitting *will* ensure *lack* of success. And that's all I know.

2. There is no "back-up plan"; there is no "day job." The logic is this — if you have a parachute, if you give yourself a way out, you will take it. People say to me, "You should always have a day job." I say NO — do not give yourself a way out! Make it so that the *only* option is to succeed.

*Wrong Turn,
Spawn,
The Marine,
Ballistic: Ecks vs.
Sever,
Tekken,
Thr3e,
Layover
(writer/director),
Left Behind,
Rapid Fire,
Halloween 4:
The Return of
Michael Myers*

ALAN MCELROY

How I start... It starts with *panic* — especially on assignments. I've somehow managed to convince a production company or studio to pay me to write a screenplay. Now, I actually have to *do it?! What the hell was I thinking? How did I do this before?* I look at old screenplays I've written and wonder, "Who wrote this? I don't remember writing this!" I pace, I clean my office, I go to my wife, Kymm, and tell her "I'm sorry, I can't do this — we're going to have to give the money back." Kymm just shakes her head and laughs, because she's heard this same dread-filled tirade over *every* screenplay I've *ever* written. It never gets any easier because every screenplay is *unique*. It has its own voice, its own pace, and its own *pulse*. That first writing *step* is always a blind risk, off a cliff into the unknown sea of *creation*. Eventually, after days of circling my desk, I finally sit down to start, usually because I have a deadline and I'm already starting to get those fateful calls, "*So, how's it going so far?*"

I start in the middle... People ask me all the time, "*How do I start my story?*" "*I can't figure out where to begin; where should I start?"* They don't know because stories don't necessarily have a true cut-and-dry beginning. For example, your life story began at your birth, right? Or did it begin with your parents nine months earlier? Or was it when they got married? Or when they first met? Or was it the incident that propelled them to meet? Or maybe it was when the Earth cooled? For me, the story already exists, like life — it has a history — a chronology. I go into the story at a critical *Moment*. Someone — the protagonist, or could be the antagonist — is facing a pivotal problem or is in the aftermath of a crucial choice, or is facing a dilemma of his or her own making, something dynamic and fundamental to who they are, that asks a Question. I will discover what led up to that *Moment* through the process of writing. What follows will invariably deal with that *Moment*, answering the Question(s) posed by that *Moment*. How does the character change, grow, find strength, find love, find inner *truth*, as he or she searches for that essential life-changing and *life-affirming* Answer? Finding that Answer *is* my story.

Once I've written that *Moment*, the panic dissolves — I am invested in this quest for an answer and in the journey of this individual. I am the chronicler. It becomes imperative for me to follow characters deep into the sea of creation, into the unknown, and let *their* story surprise me. At its best, it's no longer an *assignment*, or a *job* — it is a living, breathing universe unfolding before my eyes each day. At some point in those early pages, the *Voice* of the piece solidifies and the words come unbidden. I rush to get back there, to see what the characters are doing in that world. I eagerly talk to my wife about their exploits as though I'm discussing *people* I know, not *characters* I've created. "How did I ever do this before?" How could I not...

That's how I start...

Sherlock Holmes,
Invictus,
Don't Say a Word,
The Assassin

TONY PECKHAM

SOME OF MY FUNDAMENTALS:

Here are a few things I use; they're as important to me now, twenty-five years in, as they were at the beginning.

1. Don't be paralyzed by perfection; remember that writing is a process. You can move on from a scene, or a moment in a scene, even if it isn't exactly the way you want it to be. You can always come back and make it better. Sometimes (quite often) you'll find you didn't need what you thought you needed anyway. Just keep moving forward.

2. Stop writing while you still have something left to say. This is an old Hemingway trick. As you write every day, stop while you still know exactly what you want to put on the page, even if it's just a paragraph, or the final twist to a scene, or a sentence. That way, you never start the next day cold, facing a blank page. Very important for the long haul.

3. You don't have to write, but you can't do anything else. This is a Raymond Chandler trick. Once you've determined your premium writing time (mine is the morning), you protect that time jealously, *even from yourself*. Sit at your desk. Write, or don't write if the words aren't flowing — but don't do anything else. No email, no writing checks, no phone calls. Eventually, you get so bored that writing seems like a good alternative.

Of course, applying these requires a little discipline. But then you knew that, right? Writing is a discipline before it's an art. The art happens if you're lucky, and disciplined.

*White Men
Can't Jump*
(writer/director),
Bull Durham
(writer/director),
Tin Cup
(writer/director),
*Hollywood
Homicide*
(writer/director),
*Play It to the
Bone*
(writer/director),
*Bad Boys II,
The Great White
Hype,
Cobb*
(writer/director),
*Blue Chips,
Blaze*
(writer/director),
*The Best of Times,
Under Fire,
Dark Blue*
(director)

RON SHELTON

I need to hear the characters speak before I start writing. I want to know how they use the language to express themselves. Their voices, as well as their actions, reveal their character. Once I know how they talk, and how they talk differently from every other character, I start to know the story.

Every scene must be about forces in opposition. There is no drama unless there is conflict, and the pressure release from that conflict can be comic or tragic, but it starts and ends with conflict.

Every scene matters. There is a tendency among beginning writers to repeat themselves, to write variations on a scene instead of advancing the story. Every scene does not have to advance the plot, but it does have to advance character evolution and the story. The story is the thematic narrative you want to tell — the plot is just the mechanics. Great stories can have very little plot. Great plots don't necessarily make a good story. The story is what you take with you out of the theater, what emotional and cerebral and spiritual ride you've been on.

Second acts are the toughest because they need to continue advancing the story and raise the stakes. A second-act curtain must have raised the stakes from the first-act curtain. All great scripts are continually ratcheting up what's at risk. Third acts tend to write themselves, if the first two acts are in good shape and well structured. Third acts need to be both inevitable and surprising.

Every five-page scene I write I try to cut to four, every four-page scene to three, every three to two... tighter is better always.

A screenplay functions as a blueprint, engineering report, and rendering all at the same time. It must work for the director, the producer, the actors — AND the financier. That's the challenge.

Shutter Island,
Avatar
(executive
producer),
Pathfinder,
Alexander,
Night Watch

LAETA KALOGRIDIS

I love my job. I lie for a living, and I like to think I do it moderately well, considering the challenges of working in the film industry. What I write — a script — is part of a larger collaboration, an interim step on the way to the final product — a movie. A novel, for example, is a finished piece, standing on its own, requiring only the reader to complete the journey of the story by reading it.

A script? Not so much.

But despite this, or maybe in part because of it, I still love my job. I get to make things up all day and — this is the really incredible part — *people pay me to do it*. Enough to live on, which is a whole separate level of shocking.

I love writing itself. Even when it keeps me up until four in the morning because I can't sleep without finishing a sequence, even when it makes me miserable because I'm sure — sometimes accurately — that what I've written is completely and utterly execrable. Even when I forget to eat and don't get around to showering and make my life partner miserable. (I try not to make the kids miserable, but they can't help but notice when Mom is in the Writing Cave. It's not subtle.) I love losing myself in a line, in a page, in a story. There is nothing else in the world like it.

And when people tell me that they want to write, I always say the same things: Be ready to work. Hope for success, but be prepared for despair. Find a really good editor and listen to that person, even if he or she isn't saying what you want to hear. Center yourself in your life, not in your career, because you can have a number of the latter, but you're only getting one of the former.

And by way of clarity: Writing, to me, isn't a career, although it provides one for me. It's as much a part of life as breathing, and as necessary. I wrote compulsively and feverishly long before I ever sold something. I finished my first (mercifully unpublished) novel when I was eleven. I can't remember a time when I couldn't read, when I didn't long to write stories that I made up myself, to join along with all the authors who were my heroes as a child. If I stopped being paid tomorrow, I wouldn't stop writing. I'd just go back to the in-your-spare-time-at-dawn model that was how I lived before I started selling scripts.

As for work, success, and despair: I've often heard people come out of a movie theater, marveling at the poor quality of what they've seen, saying that they know they could work in Hollywood because they could definitely write something better than what they just saw. Arguable point — it's possible, even probable, that some of them could — but they don't realize the creative and political gauntlet the writer has to navigate just to get work, much less the way in which the currently corporatized system is stacked against most movies being any kind of artistic POV, on the part of the writer, the director, the actors, or anyone else involved.

So be ready for hard work. Very, very hard work. And that's if you're lucky enough to get hired.

Success may come; if so, try to live within your means. (Seriously, I can't give better advice than that. It's a freelance gig; don't forget it.) But a far more frequent experience is despair. A professor of mine at UCLA, Howard Suber, gives a notable lecture on the importance of being able to cope with despair. He told me, and I have never forgotten, that how people handle despair determines what sort of longevity they have in the film business. This is because despair cannot be avoided: Even the most successful among us will have things go wrong, sometimes spectacularly. And it's in those moments you'll know if you are built to keep going or not.

If you've picked up this book, you're interested in more than a career; you're interested in the inner creative life of a writer. I encourage you with all my heart: Put pen to paper, or fingers to the keys, and find out about it firsthand. Because I can't recommend the experience of writing highly enough.

I love my job. But I love writing more.

SHANE BLACK
(A SLIGHT RETURN)

STRUCTURE

Syd Field is a nice man, as is Robert McKee — and I've a special place in my heart for Michael Hague and Linda Seger, to be sure.

Having said that, here's another way of picturing the halcyon template of the THREE-ACT STRUCTURE:

Well, there's a beginning, then there's a middle, then, oddly enough — an end.

Put away your wallets; that was free.

Most folks have a sense, having seen literally hundreds of films, of things like a SETUP and PAYOFF, or, even more mysteriously, A REVERSAL.

The things that serve as guideposts in our story are moments of revelation, of surprise, where elements introduced early on in a story, things we've forgotten, come rushing to inform a scene sixty pages later, perhaps lending a chilling new context to what we're seeing.

Or, to put it simply, a bad guy says, "I hate Mooses, next time I see a f##king moose, he better watch it, etc." He even has a moose costume he uses for practice.

Then, at the end of the story, he's making his escape, when he hears a VOICE: "Hands up," spins around, mouth agape — it's THE MOOSE. With a gun. See, a COP HID inside the moose suit, so literally there's a moose now ready to shoot the GUY, tables turned.

Believe it or not? I just made that up.

In *The Hunt for Red October*, we hear Alec Baldwin twice say, "I don't smoke." But later, when everyone's at a loss with the Russians, it's Baldwin's character who asks for a cigarette — we're actually a little touched by it.

In *Kiss Kiss Bang Bang*, Harry Lockhart failed to save his childhood sweetheart when he was young enough to believe in MAGIC.

Now, at age forty, he hears her use the magic words — and becomes a true-life magician, actually WARPING the fabric of adult reality to conform to his childhood vision of what it would be.

Assignment: Next movie you see, write down the setups and payoffs. Then write down the twists and surprises, aka the REVERSALS.

ACTION MOVIES

The trouble with action movies this day is summed up by the following event.

I wanted to write a cop picture, had tried to craft a more gritty, down-and-dirty thriller than the norm… and was told it lacked scope. I agreed, actually, although I didn't know this was a bad thing until — curious now — I looked around, at tentpole film after tentpole film.

They were HUGE. They were TOO HUGE.

I realized that it's a sad state of affairs when ALL COP MOVIES NEED CGI.

Action movies, man… action is such a misnomer. It implies things hurtling through space, hitting other things, etc.

... It implies dialogue such as, "Look out," "Duck," or "You and I, Sergeant, we are very much alike."

Action sucks, I think. I don't see most action movies. Most are not, for lack of a better word, TONED. They are a continuous shout from start to finish, undifferentiated sound and fury, signifying nothing, because? Anyone who's ever fiddled with an audio equalizer knows you gotta have HIGHS and LOWS.

Who pegs all the levers at the exact same level, then cranks the volume to twelve?

Hollywood, that's who.

Now, then, action that is TONED and CLEVER? Gimme some of that, brother, I can't love you enough. The festival of pings, pops, and ka-pows that comprise the last shootout in *Butch Cassidy and the Sundance Kid*... good God, it's like a symphony torqueing itself to a crescendo. See it again.

It has RULES. Every time Sundance pulls the trigger, someone dies. It's SUBJECTIVE — you don't see everything; you feel you're locked INSIDE THE ACTION with the characters.

JAWS. You want action? Check out the lulls and crescendos here: as choreographed as any ballet, picking out the characters, again, allowing them moments WITHIN THE ACTION, allowing for shifts in pace, allowing for realizations, moves, and countermoves, sudden hope followed by desperate despair.

In a good action movie, you don't stop the drama to have action. You don't set aside character to have action. No. The action IS the drama.

The action has BEATS; it REVEALS character.

There's a horrible feeling I have that recently, in most "action" films, you can simply swap action scenes. The beginning car chase slot would, in a pinch, swap out nicely to reel six, and the climactic shootout, well, that would fill the beginning slot interchangeably. Such action scenes are events in limbo, cut off from context.

It's like everything meaningful stopped for "Action Time!" Not so *Jaws*.

Not so *La Femme Nikita*.

Not so *The French Connection*.

As far as the craft of DEPICTING action in a screenplay?

WRITING A SCRIPT TO BE READ AT THE STUDIO LEVEL

Well, here's the thing. I often feel it's more important to convey the DYNAMIC — in other words, how your action scene should FEEL and at what urgency it should play — what, in the end, we're supposed to GET from the experience.

Having said that, you describe, generally, every precise detail of what's on the screen. If it's onscreen, it ought to be in the script.

Lazy writing is, "Well, it's an abandoned amusement park, we'll figure out some sh#t when we see what's there."

No. If your action scene is to have character beats, highs and lows, suspense and scares — it better be that way on the paper.

Find the beats. Then, later, the location only serves to clarify or (it's possible) enhance the dynamic you've specified.

BREAKING THE FOURTH WALL

I always say, walk first, fly later. I got very lucky, early on, by indulging a silly need to keep myself awake at the type-writer — alluding to other movies in my scripts, arrogantly offering uncalled-for commentary on studios and showbiz, speaking candidly to the reader, etc.

I simply don't care about these comments, and if they're funny that's why. I'm just amusing myself to stay awake.

Truth is? Half of the "zingers" for which I'm credited are, in retrospect, unnecessary and embarrassing.

This notion came to fruition on *Kiss Kiss Bang Bang*, when I actually let these comments affect a jump from script to screen. And I sweated at it too much; it makes the audience annoyed — "Give us a f##king MOVIE first, then we'll decide if it's funny to comment on it, a##face."

Sometimes they wouldn't say a##face. Sentiment's the same: Don't get snide and patronizing; it just spotlights how little substance exists under all the blather.

This reaction was to be avoided. So I set myself to making a film with some weight to it, some thematic strength. Only in a bind did I resort to the wise-cracking interruptions, and then only as an extension of Harry's CHARACTER. Also? I cut out the unfunny ones, and kept the funny ones.

Can you judge whether your snide intrusions are funny or unfunny?

Most people can't be objective.

Show it to a friend. If he or she says, "Why, this is smug and unfunny," you say, "Thanks, a##face," but then proceed immediately to CUT THE BIT from the script.

Funny is good. But boy, oh, boy, is smug BAD.

Chapter **15**

INSTANT SCREENWRITING LIBRARY

When I started teaching my course at USC School of Cinematic Arts, I noted that the previous curriculum required every student to read the same book. This seemed a narrow way to accumulate information.

Instead, I assembled a list of well-regarded film industry books and made individual students each responsible for a succinct review of one book, sharing with their classmates what they considered the most impressive concepts from that work so that their peers could quickly discover books that seemed most appealing to them.

Each of us learns in different ways and each of these authors brings a unique perspective to our business — I hope these quick guides will lead you to other resources that inspire you to keep exploring.

TEN BOOKS ON WRITING, PITCHING, AND SURVIVING, AS REVIEWED BY USC FILM STUDENTS

1

THE 101 HABITS OF HIGHLY SUCCESSFUL SCREENWRITERS:
Insider Secrets from Hollywood's Top Writers
by Karl Iglesias
Publisher: Adams Media (October 2001)
Review by Jason Wong

This book is a compilation of interviews that the writer conducted with established screenwriters, which he then edited and organized into 101 mini-chapters. Each chapter uses different parts of these interviews to give insight into one facet of the craft or business of screenwriting. The book is interesting in that each of these writers has very different personalities, yet for the most part, they share the same "habits" as writers. Even more interesting are the times when some of their advice directly contradicts each other's. For me, these contradictions really hit home the point that, often, the "right" way to write is simply the way that works and allows one to produce.

The following are the ten habits I found most useful for my own writing, but keep in mind that not everyone may find these habits to be true for them:

1. **Being Collaborative** — Recognize that screenwriting is NOT like writing plays, fiction, or poetry in that your work WILL be continually shaped and reshaped by others and being willing to accept this as a constant.

2. **Being committed to a career, not just one screenplay** — The odds are stacked against you to succeed, and making money is the WRONG reason to get into screenwriting. You cannot hope to write just one good screenplay and magically have everyone want to give you money to make it and the rest of your career. You must be willing to build arduously, piece by piece.

3. **Having precise goals, not just wishes** — Be specific about what you want to achieve in a day, month, year, years. Bad planning leads to bad results.

4. **Writing down your ideas as they come** — Small ideas can be worth writing down, but can often be meaningless. Generally, big or important ideas are not easily forgotten.

5. **Outlining** — Unlike a novel or short story in which language is primary and often writers can write their

way in and out of the story, screenplays — Hollywood ones at least — are more dependent on structure, and, therefore, outlining can be key preparation so you know where you are going and don't muddle it up. The more detail you have in your outline, generally the more free you will be to discover when you are writing pages. However, some writers like to discover a few scenes at a time.

6. **Not worrying about finding ideas** — Live life and be a real human being. Take an interest in others, in the world. There are billions of good ideas and they will come to you if you are open to them.

7. **Working on several projects at one time** — really helps you to deal with rejection of a project or with writer's block on a project because it frees your mind up to not be problem-focused.

8. **Having a life** — Often, having as much time as you want to write is NOT a good thing. When you have other responsibilities, the little time you have to write can be much more productive because you don't spend it messing around.

9. **Agents** — are pointless to have if you don't have quality materials (more than one script) and the discipline to produce more of them.

10. **Perseverance** — The craft takes five to twenty years to develop. "Overnight success" comes after ten to twenty years.

2   HOW TO WRITE A MOVIE IN 21 DAYS: *The Inner Movie Method*

by Viki King
Publisher: Harper Paperbacks
(September 1993)
Review by Camila Tanabe

I had seen *How to Write a Movie in 21 Days* in bookstores before, Barnes & Nobles, maybe Borders. Every time I saw it, I'd tell myself, "This is impossible, this book should be called 'How to Write a Crappy Movie in 21 Days.'" Even a crappy script takes longer to write than twenty-one days. In the book, the writer Viki King even suggests you write no more than three hours a day. So, in choosing to read this book, I purely wanted to satisfy my (and I suppose everyone's) curiosity; what is the trick?

The basic idea turns out to be quite clever, the kind of basic common sense we wouldn't believe in until someone who has published a book tells us. She calls it "The Inner Movie Method," in which you "write from your heart; rewrite from your head." The concept is to stop juggling with the right and left brains and shut down the conscious, analytical, logical, and critical side of us and use, let's call it "instincts," to write.

The book doesn't have a great formula to help the reader do it, but to sit down and write. It gives us hints, however. The most interesting one is admitting that every time we write, we're writing about ourselves. King describes common issues, classified by age and gender, we all tend to write about, issues we all happen to have.

Once you admit you have issues and it's okay to write about them, letting go of the consciousness becomes easier and writing can flow without thought. Once that's clarified, the reader starts the actual process of writing a screenplay in, technically, twenty-one days.

It all starts with structure, when we write what King calls the nine-minute movie, or the story points that develop the plot (plot points, inciting incident, and so forth, terms that King, however, chooses not to use here). They happen on pages 1, 3, 10, 30, 45, 60, 75, 90, and 120.

Then we go into actual writing in blocks of ten to thirty pages at a time: no thinking, just writing. Then we rewrite also in blocks of around fifteen pages at a time. And finally we tweak, act by act.

The book closes with a fifty-page pep talk, of how "yes, you can do it," with tips on being a writer and owning your "writerhood," how to deal with time management, getting bills paid, having self-confidence, killing procrastination, understanding psychological hypochondria to avoid writing, and sticking to your dreams.

It finally ends by giving us a quick idea of how to get screenplays sold/produced/read. Overall, even though effective in theory, the book seems to be directed to first-time writers.

I truly believe good scripts can be born with King's method, but I still fail to believe there is such a thing as "the method" in writing. *How to Write a Movie in 21 Days* has tips, some funny jokes, some not-so-funny jokes, some great ideas, powerful insights on self-discovery, and generic pep talks, but no solution or magical formulas.

TEN KEY (OR INTERESTING) POINTS

1. **"Ideas are the only thing inflation hasn't hit.** They're still a dime a dozen. It's what you do with your ideas that gives them value."

2. **The Inner Movie Method**: "Write from your heart; rewrite from your head."

3. **Movies themes often fall into "Writes of Passage."** The story you write will be a metaphor for your life. It means that the life issue that most concerns you now "will be explored in your writing... If you're only working something out for a fictional character who doesn't exist in some part of you, then it isn't worth it."

4. **Who you are**: personality, age, issues and scars, gender; everything dictates what issues you'll write about.

5. **The 9-Minute Movie**: creating structure by writing first the nine pages that represent the keys points of the plot. On page 1, mood, tone, and place are given. On page 3, the central question of the movie is presented. Page 10 is where the story is presented. Page 30 introduces an event that will move the protagonist into new territory. On page 45, we see initial growth in the character. Page 60 is where the protagonist makes a commitment to what he or she wants. On page 75, the protagonist reaches bottom and all seems lost, but something changes him or her. Page 90 is the beginning of the resolution, and by page 120, the audience is satisfied with the resolution given to the story that was promised on page 10.

6. **"Don't think too much about your movie:** The longer you take; the longer you'll take."

7. **The schedule to write a movie in twenty-one days is as follows:** Day 1: Write 10 pages; Day 8: Rest; Day 15: Rewrite pages 75 to 90; Day 2: Write pages 10 to 30; Day 9: Read the first draft; Day 16: Rewrite pages 90 to 100; Day 3: Write pages 30 to 45; Day 10: Rewrite pages 1 to 10; Day 17: Rewrite pages 100 to 120; Day 4: Write pages 45 to 60; Day 11: Rewrite pages 10 to 30; Day 18: Tweak Act 1; Day 5: Write pages 60 to 75; Day 12: Rewrite pages 30 to 45; Day 19: Tweak Act 2; Day 6: Write pages 75 to 90; Day 13: Rewrite pages 45 to 60; Day 20: Tweak Act 3; Day 7: Write pages 90 to 120; Day 14: Rewrite pages 60 to 75; Day 21: Celebrate.

8. **Basic ideas concerning the first read and rewriting:** Don't judge; check if scenes work, if ideas are conveyed clearly, if there's a more efficient way to tell something; ask yourself if this is the story you wanted to tell; compare the movie you wanted to write to the one you actually did.

9. **Things to look for while tweaking:** Look for holes in the plot; answer questions that need to be answered; check if cause and effect builds, if setups are paid off; tighten the first ten pages; make sure the dialogue is clear; recheck if the central life questions are clear; sum up descriptions in one word, if possible; make jokes funnier, if it's a comedy; check if exposition is too in the face.

10. **"Obstacles are only there in case you care to stop."**

3

SAVE THE CAT!: The Last Book on Screenwriting You'll Ever Need
by Blake Snyder
Publisher: Michael Wiese Productions
        (May 2005)
Review by Douglas Jessup

Blake Snyder's *Save the Cat!* isn't your typical instruction manual for constructing the screenplay. Instead of boring readers into a catnap (get it: "cat" nap) with endless technical jargon and lackluster diagrams, Snyder provides his audience with an entertaining, fresh, and extremely insightful approach to conquering the challenges of the screenwriting process. While some writers don't preach outlines or a lot of preparation, Snyder deems it completely mandatory. He provides important exercises that will get your story fleshed out so that when it comes time to actually sit down and write, you can do just that — sit down and write, instead of wondering what to type next. The second half of the book concentrates on what to do after you've written your first draft. He provides great advice on how to avoid textbook story blunders that trivialize your plot, how to fix weak points that are haunting you, and how to get your script sold. Filled with great one-liners and relevant anecdotes acquired over his extremely successful writing career, *Save the Cat!* provides a truly pleasurable learning experience. It is a quick read that I would recommend any aspiring screenwriter read *at least* once.

BRILLIANT POINTS

1. **ALWAYS START with a perfect logline and a killer title.** Four components of a great logline are irony, mental image, audience, and cost. Pitch your idea to strangers: must hook them in one or two sentences.

2. **Ten genres that all movies fall into.** Identify which genre your story belongs to, watch other movies within that genre, find the patterns (both the ones that work and those that don't). "Make it the same, only different": stick to the blueprint of your genre, while avoiding the clichés.

3. **It's about a guy who...** The who has to serve the "what is it?" question. In other words, the hero has to enhance the theme of the story. What type of person would have the farthest to travel, the greatest obstacles to overcome, and the most conflict in the situation? The hero, like the story, must be primal: have basic wants, needs, and desires. Make sure the logline reflects this.

4. **Snyder Beat Sheet: 15 plot points that every screenplay must have** (included). It lists what page(s) they should fall on or within.

5. **The BOARD: Master the beats of your story with this visual aid.** Divides your story into four equal parts: Act 1; Act 2 first half, Act 2 second half; and Act 3. Place, rearrange, and whittle down forty note cards that represent the forty scenes of your story (ten note cards for each part). This coincides with the Snyder Beat Sheet.

6. **Snappy Rules for Screenwriting.** Save the Cat: Make the hero likable early on in the story to invest the audience. Pope in the Pool: Bury the exposition in an interesting scene that will help keep viewers interested while exposing important backstory. Double Mumbo Jumbo: Include only one piece of magic per script; in *Signs*, for example, aliens and God were too much to handle. Laying Pipe: Too much setup is bad; you risk losing the audience. Black Vet: Don't overdo the irony. Watch Out. Glacier: Make danger *present, literally*. Arc: Every character must arc (at least all the main ones). Keep the Press Out: Putting the media in a story pulls the magic out of it.

7. **The Fixes.** The Hero Leads: The protagonist must lead and be active. Talking The Plot: Use action, not dialogue to advance the plot. Badder Bad Guy: If your protagonist isn't cutting it, make the villain worse. Turn. Turn. Turn: Accelerate the plot as the story progresses. Color Wheel: Life isn't just one single emotion; movies shouldn't be either. Hi. How Are You: Stale, everyday dialogue is bad and boring. Limp/Eyepatch: Make EVERY character unique. Primal: Is the conflict primal? Does it appeal to concrete human instincts?

8. **Networking in person is better than a call; a call is better than a cover letter: a cover letter is better than an email.** Pitch your script at film festivals, meet other up-and-coming writers at screenwriting classes, join a screenwriters group, try writing as a movie critic to gain some notoriety. Avoid screenwriting contests — very rarely does this do anything for your career. Don't post an ad in *Variety* with your picture and a caption that says "will write for food."

4

LEW HUNTER'S SCREENWRITING
434: The Industry's Premier Teacher Reveals the Secrets of the Successful Screenplay
by Lew Hunter
Publisher: Perigree Trade, Revised Edition
(May 2004)
Review by Nick Wenger

Lew Hunter describes his book best: "What I'm trying to convey are the basic rules. Not Lew Hunter's rules but the rules of screen history stretching back to the American invention of motion pictures by Thomas Edison… It is wildly important to first learn the rules, before you start bending or breaking them."

Based on a graduate course he teaches at UCLA's School of Theater, Film and Television, Hunter breaks down the basics of writing a Hollywood screenplay. He first analyzes the classic story structure of Aristotle and Plato, giving special attention to the importance of the story "idea" above all else. He breaks down development, act structure, dialogue tricks, comedy, and various other aspects of writing. He maintains a very positive outlook, and it makes for an entertaining and inspiring read. Throughout the book, Hunter creates a hypothetical movie called "The Glass Hammer" as an example for each screenwriting step. We follow the script from conception through rewrite. Additionally, he makes consistent reference to five major films, which he feels best embody modern screenwriting: *E.T.*, *Casablanca*, *Butch Cassidy*, *Citizen Kane*, and *Fallen Angel* (a TV movie).

BULLET POINTS

1. **All good stories are based on sex or violence.** This can be expressed socially, as opposed to physically, for example, as the violence of social abuse or sexual tension. In *E.T.*, life/death is the primary driving force for the little alien. Hunter cites several examples that consistently fit the mold.

2. **You should be able to tell your story in two pages,** double-spaced, what Hunter calls the "two minute movie." Within it, you should have your beginning, middle, and end, as you would in a verbal story. It should make the audience care, and it should have a spine rooted in reality. From there, you can create your entire film.

3. **The do's and don'ts in dialogue include:**
   a. Don't worry about writing completely realistic dialogue, because it can be distracting or irritating. What matters is the illusion of reality.
   b. Don't write obscure dialogue that will ostracize your audience.
   c. Hide exposition in action or comedy, or through very subtle dialogue.

4. **The 180 Degree Rule means that you can turn story-development or dialogue on its head by deliberately going in the opposite direction of what is obvious.** If the line should be "I love you," make it "I hate you." Keep the audience guessing.

5. **Third-act writing is often overlooked and under-appreciated, even in well-respected films**. It should be the ultimate climax, tearing at the emotion of the audience. Hunter argues that a movie like *Rain Man*, though good, would have been much better if the third act had been more extreme and more emotional. He argues that the movie just "ends," with Dustin Hoffman getting on a train and Tom Cruise blankly watching. This was a failed opportunity to move the audience on a grander scale.

6. **Finishing your first draft is a paramount achievement** that will lay the foundation for a long journey of rewrites. Once you have finished your first draft, you will be ecstatic for a short period, and then it will hit you: the "Afterbirth Blues." This is the stage in which you feel empty and bare, because you aren't 100% happy with your story, and you're afraid the world will tear it apart. Don't stress it, just avoid negative criticism, and rewrite until you're no longer afraid to share your baby.

5

PITCHING HOLLYWOOD: How to Sell Your TV and Movie Ideas

by Jonathan Koch and Robert Kosberg
with Tanya Meurer Norman
Publisher: Linden Publishing (April 2004)
Review by Alex Pickering

Pitching Hollywood is a "how-to" book about pitching ideas to Hollywood by two Hollywood "pitchmen" and producers, Jonathan Koch and Robert Kosberg. The book is divided into chapters that cover many stages of the pitching process: the actual inception of an idea and all the researching and litmus testing that comes with that, the fashioning and honing of a pitch, and the marketing measures to get one's foot in the door.

Throughout the book, Jonathan and Bob (as they prefer to be called) often inject anecdotes or tidbits from their own experiences into the material for each subject. At times, they may even share a sort of back-and-forth banter about a particular topic. Initially, they explain who they are and how they created their positions. After explaining the difference between "high concept" pitches and the less sellable ones, they provide examples of various pitches. The book proceeds to explain ways to prepare one's pitch and take the necessary steps to get in-office meetings. Jonathan and Bob also describe what to do once you are in the room, as well as offer a number of examples of high-concept synopses and treatments in the final chapter.

TEN MAIN POINTS

1. **Finding ideas through photocopying.** According to Jonathan and Bob, there are incredible story ideas to be found in newspapers. The art of photocopying and optioning rights from these sources is an important skill to hone.

2. **The ideas of the "everyman."** You must be what the authors call an "idea person," always seeking sad, uplifting, tragic, ironic, or funny ideas from all around, including from family members, acquaintances, and strangers. Especially profitable are experiences from people outside of L.A., bringing new material to the producers of Southern California. Hollywood needs the "everyman."

3. **High concept vs. low concept.** High-concept ideas give you the meat of the story in one to two sentences and have their own legs to carry them up the tiers of production. Low-concept ideas, conversely, may be great and Academy Award–worthy, but they are more difficult to pitch and sell.

4. **Knowing if you have a good idea.** Ideas need to be fresh, commercially viable, marketable, timely, and applicable to key demographics.

5. **Determine the value of ideas.** Be sure to know what you want from the sale of your idea — money, credit, a job, or maybe even a combination of all three.

6. **Protect your idea.** Register your treatment. Also, remember that the higher the concept, the tighter the pitch and the catchier the logline (Jonathan and Bob's example being "*Jaws* with paws"). Such a pitch is harder for someone to steal because it has such a specific flavor.

7. **Prepare your pitch.** Give the project a catchy working title. Write a treatment if it helps you work out your pitch (as well as enables you to register it with the WGA). Condense your treatment onto one page and practice it with yourself, family, and friends.

8. **Get yourself in the room.** Make hundreds of phone calls. Send hundreds of emails and/or faxes. Do whatever you can to get in the office. Subscribe to or buy a copy of the *Hollywood Creative Directory* or the *Producers 411* to find the contact information of the producers and executives that pertain to your project idea. Above all, be persistent. Get the assistant's name so that next time you call you speak on a more personal level. Be respectful and ask for just fifteen minutes of the target producer or executive's time.

9. **What to do once you're in the room.** Be on time. Sign the "Studio Release Agreement." Show that you are aware of the studio or production company's current and past projects and successes. Be enthusiastic, confident, and collaborative. Don't rush. Also, if you can, don't leave any material behind.

10. **Be patient during the development period.** Often you have little or no control over your idea once you sell it, so just move on to the next idea. Your project may be shelved or never happen. It's the way it works.

6

500 WAYS TO BEAT THE HOLLYWOOD SCRIPT READER:
Writing the Screenplay the Reader Will Recommend

by Jennifer Lerch
Publisher: Fireside (July 1999)
Review by Jeanette McDuffie

Movie studios and production companies receive tens of thousands of screenplays each year, and executives can't read them all. They use readers to sift through and recommend screenplays. The reader communicates all the essential points of a screenplay in a concise document. It's the unofficial *Cliff Notes* of your screenplay. It is important that you write to sell, paying attention to the screenplay's appearance, concept, characters, and structure.

MAIN POINTS

1. **The coverage report usually has four parts:** a concept line, a synopsis, a comments page that analyzes strengths and weaknesses, and a graph that shows where your characters, story, dialogue, and structure rate.

2. **A reader may judge the script just by its general appearance**, so make sure it is professional and conforms to industry standards. The professional screenwriter conforms to a few basic standards: proper dialogue margins, screenplay length (100 to 120 pages). Script copies should be crisp and clean on high-quality paper and bound with two or three strong brads. Use your screenplay cover for title, your name, and contact information. Do not include any other information in the script like the budget, your resume, or dream cast.

3. **The typical Hollywood reader only sees your script.** The only way that readers understand the story you're trying to tell is through the screenplay itself. Engage them with your setting, characters, and style. Do a good job of scripting the setting to pull the readers out of their office and into your story. The more unique the setting, the greater your chance of pulling readers into the screenplay. Make every detail count, and show instead of tell. Choose a setting that will aggravate your protagonist's problems. Including the right details is essential in bringing the characters to life. Make physical traits general but vivid. Show their private internal conflicts in dramatic, visual ways. Make sure the character's actions and dialogue remain consistent. Consistency is a hallmark of professional writing. Dialogue should be fresh and sound like you took it straight out of the characters' mouths. It should not be too on the nose or too predictable. Include levels of meaning in what your characters say to each other. Explore the style that top writers employ. It should be lean, economical, and clear. Convey the essence of what happens onscreen in a few well-chosen words. You are writing to communicate a total experience that translates to the screen. Write in word pictures that are vivid, succinct, and precise. Make sure action sequences are exciting, conversational, and logical.

4. **Create a concept and characters that will sell your script.** The essence of your story has to be summed up in a few catchy words or phrases. A few tips:

   a. It could be a high-concept story that has a catchy idea and broad appeal.

   b. Create a concept around an issue we can root for passionately and personalize it.

   c. Build into your concept a hero whose weakness makes achieving the goal difficult.

   d. Tap into human experiences like love, loss, revenge, or coming of age.

   e. Play into a familiar circumstance that takes a bizarre or ironic turn.

   f. Tweak a clichéd concept by adding a unique setting. Think not what the star can do for your script, but what the script can do for your star. Authentic, original characters can get industry power players interested in your story. Ten ways to make characters spring to life:

   ▸ Give them a world view.

   ▸ Assign idiosyncrasies.

   ▸ Develop backstories.

   ▸ Integrate attitudes and values towards things.

   ▸ Give characters a home.

   ▸ Give characters a dark side.

   ▸ Characters need flaws.

   ▸ Characters who are not prepared for what happens keep the reader rooting for them.

5. **Certain things must happen at certain points** in your screenplay or the reader will feel dissatisfied.

6. **The first part of your screenplay should hook the reader fast** and not let go. Establish the story's genre. Create a compelling situation. Introduce the protagonist

and antagonist and set up subplots. Establish your character's conflict in the opening scenes. Let the readers know what they're rooting for and foreshadow where the story is going. Many of the best scripts start fast. Don't spend the first pages on backstory. Feed the readers your character's history through the story structure, piece by piece. At the end of the first act, you should be twenty to thirty pages into the screenplay.

7. **Conflict is the most important component** of your screenplay. Something must be at stake that the reader cares about. The conflict should be compelling, juicy, and fresh. As you evaluate your central conflict, know that great conflicts explore universal themes and relationships.

8. **Good Act 2 structure keeps the story moving forward** so the reader has a reason to stay interested. Act 2 focuses on the main problem from Act 1 but gradually builds tension and builds momentum. Broaden the story's conflict and include major complications. Test your script by writing a synopsis in the same way a reader would. Hit the main beats, surprises, reversals, points of no return, climax, and resolution. There should be at least four major sequences in this act that each contain their own goals and opposition and rhythm. The sequences should feel seamless. They should each address the central conflict. To communicate character growth, think of the growth as a gong. Every ten to fifteen pages, you want to bang the gong. It will weave into the story a sense that the character is consistently growing. Keep the reader guessing — complicate the life of the protagonist, give false clues, reveal clues slowly, throw emotional and physical obstacles in the way. End Act 2 with a strong "all is lost" scenario.

7

BREAKFAST WITH SHARKS: A Screenwriter's Guide to Getting the Meeting, Nailing the Pitch, Signing the Deal, and Navigating the Murky Waters of Hollywood
by Michael Lent
Publisher: Three Rivers Press (May 2004)
Review by Corey Bodoh-Creed

Breakfast with Sharks gives a rough, broad overview of the business of screenwriting. The author, Michael Lent, spends a good portion of the book speaking about how a career is born, discussing such topics as the pros and cons of relocating to Los Angeles, and the various positions that can be held at the bottom of the industry totem pole that still allow time for writing. Lent also describes the business of spec and assignment work, offers advice on handling rejection, and recommends the best places to network, but writes mostly about how to deal with executives, agents, managers, producers, actors, and directors without really detailing how meetings with said important individuals are ever acquired or how to perform in these meetings once they are scheduled.

PRIMARY POINTS

1. **When meeting with important people, try to turn rejection or delays around in your favor** by saying something to the effect of, "You mentioned that the final decision on my spec is up to the senior VP, and that's cool. In the meantime, if you have anything you want someone to crack, I'd love a shot."

2. **Pitches should be prepared so that they can be expanded or contracted at a moment's notice,** depending on whether the executives seem bored or eager to hear more.

3. **Spec sales generate higher levels of income than assignments**, but competition over assignments is fierce because of the relative security they afford, in that the writer is being paid and the project is more likely to be produced.

4. **Appear to be flexible when pitching.** Executives, producers, and directors will test your openness to notes, so an excitement for their ideas should be displayed, even if it is inauthentic.

5. **Managers help develop material**, whereas agents are solely interested in selling it.

6. **Agents are a must-have for career advancement** because they are the gatekeepers to the industry. They will drop you if you do not generate enough income quickly enough.

7. **Before going to a meeting, find out as much as you can about the other person** so that you know their tastes and how hard they work. For example, an actor may have a first-look deal at a studio, but might only purchase the occasional script with discretionary funds to keep the staff busy enough so that the studio will continue to pay for the upkeep of the office.

8. **Notes are given by virtually everyone** and are expected to be heeded, but the writer must also be able to determine which notes are viable and able to explain why others are not.

9. **It is often better not to have representation than to have bad representation** or representation that does not care about you or your career.

10. **The bottom can drop out from a deal at any time,** so it is important to prepare for the worst.

8

THE HOLLYWOOD RULES: What You Must Know to Make It in the Film Industry

by Anonymous
Publisher: Fade In (January 2000)
Review by Justin Feldman

Ever wish you could sit down with Lou Wasserman, Steven Spielberg, Orson Welles, and Robert Evans and learn every trick they ever came across to make it big? These shortcuts to success are exactly what the author of *The Hollywood Rules* sets out to define. With regard to the ever-changing landscape that is the Hollywood film industry, the book begs the question: "Can there be laws within a lawless society?" The author, who remains anonymous, infers that there are indeed "rules" within the industry. Moreover, the book insists that these little known caveats are more like guidelines that should be followed at all costs. The book is written mostly for aspiring writers and producers, and deals with topics including idea conception, finding an agent/manager/lawyer, selling your project (without getting screwed), and even proper etiquette at Hollywood parties. All in all, the author seems willing to bestow his or her accumulated knowledge on the heads of up-and-coming talents in order to ensure one thing: that we make good films.

The Hollywood Rules reads more like a cross between a stereo instruction manual and a self-help book like *How to Win Friends and Influence People*. The thirty basic rules are each explained in plain English, and the author even relates some anecdotes demonstrating how the rules are obeyed by the successes and ignored by the failures.

For instance, when discussing rule number 21, "Ask for Everything," the author brings up the case of a hot music video director who was asked to helm a feature for a studio. The author explains that rather than asking for everything, this fool demanded everything, and was quickly replaced on the project. The lesson of the rule: Ask for everything because you deserve it, but if you demand it the studio gods will smite you where you stand.

Since Hollywood is such a complex place and relationships can be very fickle here, the rules are more like handy little tips that can help you on your path. Some of the tips seem like common sense, such as don't be a pest when you're waiting to hear about a possible project. Other "rules" in the book seem less practical, like showing others that you are both focused on specifics and have an independent mind by asking for a specific soft drink in a meeting. Still, many of the "rules," especially the ones regarding the business practices of entertainment, are very helpful to a layperson. In addition, the book's very matter-of-fact style reads quickly and makes you think that you're sitting across from a mentor — like a dirty version of Dicky Fox from *Jerry Maguire*.

Each rule is usually built on the one before it, so they are all meant to be used together as a cohesive Hollywood lifestyle guide. The book explains that by putting the rules into practice you can increase your chances of succeeding in Hollywood. Notice I said increase your chances, not guarantee. Towards the end of the book the author deftly brings up the idea that nothing in Tinseltown is guaranteed (unless you've got it in writing). There is no substitute for luck. But the writer does imply that if you follow the rules, you may become so hot in Hollywood that luck will seek you out. Then again, the second-to-last rule is, "Keep the Karma Gods Happy."

9 SELLING YOUR STORY IN 60 SECONDS: The Guaranteed Way to Get Your Screenplay or Novel Read

by Michael Hauge
Publisher: Michael Wiese Productions
(October 2006)
Review by Brent McHenry

Written by expert screenwriting consultant and coach, Michael Hauge, *Selling Your Story in 60 Seconds: The Guaranteed Way To Get Your Screenplay or Novel Read* is a clear and concise guide to pitching and selling a story for writers and screenwriters of all experience levels. Written in easy-to-understand terms, Hauge's book breaks down the entire process of selling your story — including the ten key components of a commercial story, how to design a strong pitch, targeting the right buyer, securing opportunities to pitch, and what steps to take next if a potential buyer says yes or no. As a how-to guide filled with industry tips, techniques, tricks, and etiquette guidelines, it's an invaluable tool for any writer trying to break into the business.

While he doesn't offer information about the three-act format, character arcs, and story beats, Hauge succeeds in dealing with all the details of the sell itself. He lays out in-depth instructions on how to figure out what it is you want to sell; whom you want to approach; the avenues, means, and methods of approaching them; the sixty-second pitch; and the aftermath.

Lastly, he dedicates 40 of the 180 pages in the book to advice and opinions of experienced Hollywood executives, who each explain what works and doesn't work during a pitch. Told from the insider's perspective, this proves to be a very effective and refreshing aspect of the book. In the end, *Selling Your Story in 60 Seconds: The Guaranteed Way to Get Your Screenplay or Novel Read* is a fantastic, fully informative, easy read that delivers the essential elements at the core of the sixty-second pitch.

MAIN POINTS

1. **The 60-second pitch** (or the telephone pitch, elevator pitch, or pitch-fest pitch). This book is about selling. But it's not really about selling your screenplay or novel. It's about selling someone the opportunity to read your story — how to convince potential agents and buyers to spend their most valuable asset — their time — in exchange for the personal and financial riches your story will bring.

2. **The cardinal rule of pitching.** The single biggest mistake writers make in pitching their work is that they try to tell their story. In other words, writers have only a minute (or maybe up to five if they're lucky) to convince a buyer to look at their book or screenplay. So talking as fast as they can, writers launch into the opening scene, then go on to detail step by step the plot of the story. There's simply no way to do justice to the plot of a novel or feature-length film in that amount of time. So what can you do if you can't tell the full story? Simply put, you get the buyer to read your manuscript

or screenplay by getting him or her to feel something positive about it.

3. **The primary objective of all story.** The goal of every screenplay, every movie, every novel, every story of any kind (and, ultimately, every work of art) is identical: to elicit emotion. We go to the movies and read books so we can feel something positive or fulfilling, something we can't feel as much or as intensely in our everyday lives. The storyteller's job is to create that feeling for the mass audience. When you pitch your story, you must provide buyers with a positive emotional experience, and you must convince them that your story will create an even stronger emotional experience for the people who will buy tickets and books and DVDs.

4. **Like it or not, the 60-second pitch is a sales pitch.** You're asking potential buyers to invest their time and money representing or producing or publishing your story. The only way you'll get them to do that is if they believe that the end result will be a big profit. In other words, your goal is to get your buyers to think, "This is a movie I'd like to see," or more important, "This is a story that will make a lot of money."

5. **Ultimately, the writer must select the elements of the story that will excite potential buyers** and make them eager to get their hands on the writer's work before anyone else does. The writer must present those key elements to the right people, in a manner so compelling they can't say no.

6. **The 8 steps to a powerful pitch (The 8 R's of Pitching).**

   Review: You must examine your story to determine its most powerful elements — the qualities you'll reveal in your pitch.

Write: After selecting the key elements to include in your pitch, you must prepare a script of exactly what you're going to say.

Rehearse: You must practice and practice your pitch, then rewrite it and practice it some more.

Research: While you're completing your screenplay or novel and preparing your pitch, you'll also be targeting your market. Compile a list of the specific buyers that you're going to pursue.

Rapport: As soon as you contact or meet a buyer, you must establish a personal relationship — before you begin talking about your story.

Revelation: When you finally launch your pitch, you must reveal the strongest, most emotionally involving information about yourself and your project you can.

Request: Once you've outlined your story, you have to ask the buyer to read it.

Response: An effective pitch means listening, not just talking. You must respond to the buyers' comments, questions, and requests, both to increase their interest and to strengthen your relationship with them.

10 THE SCRIPT-SELLING GAME:
A Hollywood Insider's Look at Getting
Your Script Sold and Produced
by Kathie Fong Yoneda
Publisher: Michael Wiese Productions
(May 2002)
Review by Lea W. Dizon

A very good book that's easy to read, *The Script-Selling Game* is packed with information and practical tips to aid new writers — in particular, how to play the script-selling game and possibly win. It looks thick but can be read in one sitting. The entire book can be summarized in three major points:

1. **Be Prepared.** Like a good story, you don't know what will happen next. So be prepared.

   a. That means constantly having a great idea ready all the time.

      ▶ Ask What if _____? Magically transport your readers to another world by filling in the blanks of this phrase. For example, what if a young boy, worried about his lonely widowed father, called a national talk show for advice?

(*Sleepless in Seattle*). What if a ragtag group of un-employed Brits threw caution to the wind and decided to "bare it all" in order to earn some money as well as gain self-respect? (*Full Monty*).

▸ Read books, newspapers, and magazines.

▸ Go to the airport or ride a bus and watch people.

▸ Watch movies, even the movies that don't necessarily appeal to you.

b. Always be prepared to pitch. You might have to pitch anytime, anywhere, even if you don't want to. Pitching is the necessary evil if you want your script sold. Be ready to have different versions of your pitch to your story:

▸ If you suddenly encounter Clint Eastwood in an elevator or George Lucas at a festival party, you can tell your story in less than a minute.

▸ Have a POP or pitch on paper. This is the elevator pitch on paper. This goes on any query letter you send out. Always have a brief treatment ready, too, as well as a release form accompanying this.

▸ The big pitch: For meetings, have a concise pitch that's five to seven minutes long. The big pitch is the "verbal trailer" of the film. It should have the highlights of the film and the description of the characters. Have a backup pitch in case you're asked for other ideas.

c. Practice, practice, practice your pitch, short or long. Just practice it in front of a mirror and in front of an audience, before you go to a party or a big meeting. Show style and confidence.

d. Being prepared also means doing your research in order to position yourself and your story well.

▸ What do producers or the studios want? Who is their target audience? What genre is their specialty? What do they know about you? How did they hear about you, if they are asking for a meeting?

▸ Do research on your script. Pay strict attention to detail. Is your script a high-production script, which could affect the budget? (Where are the locations? Are there children? Big stunts? The period?) Are your characters interesting? Does it have a clear arc? Do you need all the scenes? Can you tell your story in three, even two, sentences? Who is your target audience? Does your script grab attention within the first fifteen to twenty pages? Are you giving enough details to paint the story well? Or are you giving too much? Do you have too much dialogue? Is it fresh and insightful?

▸ Research contests and fellowships that are available. Read the trades. Read the gossip columns. Be vigilant in looking for opportunities to position yourself to sell your script.

2. **Learn the language.** Here is some industry jargon that a writer needs to learn:

   ▸ **High Concept** — commercial enough for a mass audience.

   ▸ **Low Concept** — a narrowly focused movie that will have a more limited mass appeal.

   ▸ **MOW (movie of the week)** — movie meant for TV or cable.

   ▸ **Unsolicited** — material that comes to a studio, agency, or production company without representation.

   ▸ **Ten-percenter** — the commission agents make when they sell a writer's work.

- ▸ **Packaging** — putting the talent and the financing with the script.
- ▸ **Housekeeping Deal** — when a studio provides a production company with an office and small staff. In exchange, the company is required to take its projects to that studio first before taking them anywhere else. This deal is also referred to as a "First-Look Deal."
- ▸ **Pasadena** — if a script analyst rejects or passes on a project.
- ▸ **30/10 Read** — when a script fails to hook a reader after the first thirty pages, and only the last ten pages are read.
- ▸ **Page-oner** — a rewrite from page one.
- ▸ **Boffo** — a box-office success.
- ▸ **Back-end Participation** — percentage of the profits that someone gets after the film has been released.
- ▸ **The Coverage** — the concise, accurate retelling of the main storyline and subplots, accompanied by the comments on the material and the writing style.

KNOW THE PROCESS: Log in. Coverage report. Thumbs up. Thumbs down. Positive pass. Waiting game. Development. Green light. Red light. It's important to find someone who can also speak this language for you and represent you. Look for an agent, find a manager, and create a relationship with an entertainment lawyer.

3. **It's all about relationships.** Do not underestimate the power of assistants. It's a small town. Word gets around. Attend workshops. Have a writer's support group. Network, network, network.

Chapter 16

INSPIRATIONS
AND EXPLORATIONS

PLAYFUL WAYS TO APPROACH EACH CHAPTER AND OPEN UP YOUR THINKING

1. PASSION

When you were a child you could find passion in the most simple things just by bringing your imagination into play and spending unlimited time both inside and outside yourself.

As we become adults we often question our rights to our passions. We worry that they are silly, selfish, or even inappropriate. "Hey Van Gogh — just paint the damn thing, enough with the splotching!"

As a writer, give yourself the right to explore your curiosity, instincts, and passions.

Write down this simple statement and sign it.

This is my personal declaration of independence.
I have the right to a creative life! Artistic liberty! The pursuit of passion and happiness, and the right to create anything I can imagine!

Signed _____

2. WHY DO WE WATCH MOVIES?

Go to a movie theater (choose a film similar in genre to a script you intend to write). Sit near the front, off to one side. Quietly turn and observe your fellow audience (as much as your neck can take). Watch the audience members' faces as they become immersed in the film.

You will see for yourself when the movie is working; the audience is entranced. Observe the amazing synchrony between the viewers' emotions and the characters' on the screen.

3. YES, BUT CAN I WRITE?

Sometimes we have a firm, clear knowledge of what we want to write. But, often, stories need some help to find us. Decide to be a good host; free up a few hours of your time for your inspirations to visit.

Break your daily habits, change your physical environment, take a walk on a beach, sit in a park. Visit a rooftop lookout, a museum, a zoo, a graveyard. Whatever environment changes your emotional track, give yourself this time; it is an investment.

Inspiration isn't a scientific process. It is mysterious and magical. It's mind fishing: We can lower the line, but we can't know what is going to be pulled to the surface until it bites.

Carry a method to make notes — a pad and pen, a voice memo, a video camera, whatever works for you.

Develop your eccentricity. You are taking your brain for a test drive. Listen to music. Create in silence. Write when others sleep. Dress in the same clothes every day. Pray or pace. A system that helps your ideas form may be crazy to another. But… if it works?!

There is no wrong way to create.

Just for fun try this:

PEN'S PLOT PLAYGROUND

On this and the next page are three categories of inciting words.

CHARACTERS - STYLE - SETTINGS

Let your eyes roam over the categories, combining a line or more from each, in any order. You might be surprised as your unconscious mind tries to impose order.

Note any ideas for stories that appeal to you as you make combinations.

CHARACTER		
Coward	Cinderella	Super Wealthy
Possessed	Bitch	Child Prodigy
Cursed	Artist	Innovator
Undead	Rivals	Murderer
Medical	Grandmother	Abused
Cheat	Magician	Wiseman
Criminal	Gay/Lesbian/ Transgender	Racer
Peacemaker		Zealot
Mother	Inventor/Genius	Innocent Person
Rebel	Reluctant Hero/ Leader	Captive/Slave
Rivals	Martyr	Jealous
Teacher	Strange Child	Conqueror
Discoverer	Doctor	Repairer
Farmer		Nurse/Care Giver
Psychosis	Robot/Created Person	Selfish/Jealous
Superpower	Deformed/ Crippled/ Tiny Lovers	Spy
Bully		Saint
Investigator	Adolescent	

STYLE		
Ghost Story	Romance	Love not Sex
Science Fiction	Race	Sex not Love
Thriller	Anthropomorphized Animals	Flashback
Horror/Scary		Loyalty/Honor
Fantasy	Teen Sex	Quest
Fish out of Water	Role Reversal	War
Survival	Child's View	Bearing Burden
Pratfall Comedy	Treasure Seeker	Ethnic
Legal	Justice	Spiritual
Western	Monster	Noir
Biography	Fairy Tale	Tear Jerker
Detective	Child's Story	Ecological
Bible Story	Animation	
Musical	Courage	

SETTINGS		
World of Science	Holy Land	Death Sentence
Supernatural World	Future	Famine
Unique Culture	Sweeping Change	A Remote Village
War	Past	A Vast City
Lost Somewhere	Deprivation	Another Planet
Disaster	Enchanted world	Underwater
Woman's World	Social Change	Last Survivors
Family	Prison	Very Old People
Addiction	Lower Class/Poor	Young Un-ready People
Sports	Aftermath	
Endurance Race	Terrible Weather	Seasonal Holiday
Constant Danger	Hospital	Show Business
Man's World	Hatred	

4. NOBODY KNOWS ANYTHING!

Can you name some of the biggest Hollywood flops of all time?

No one sets out to make a bad movie, but every one of these films got financed by the same kind of people who may be rejecting your projects:

a) *Lucas reportedly spent $2 million on the duck suit.*

b) *Before a single frame of film had been shot, TriStar shelled out a cool million to construct da Vinci's gold machine.*

c) *Warren Beatty and Dustin Hoffman insult the memory of the Bob Hope-Bing Crosby "Road" movies.*

d) *John Travolta plays a dreadlocked, platform-shoed 7-foot alien baddie named Terl, who was "groomed from birth to conquer galaxies."*

e) *The actress received an unheard-of million-dollar payday to essay the Queen of the Nile, a fee that reportedly ballooned to $7 million with all the overtime.*

f) *The out-of-control and unsupervised Cimino shot and re-shot. The egomaniacal auteur, whose contract stipulated that the film be no longer than three hours, ended up shooting 1.5 million feet of film, enough for several feature-length movies. The original cut clocked in at nearly four hours and was eviscerated by critics.*

g) *A grateful nation repays the messiah-like postal worker by erecting a massive statue in his image.*

h) *Michael Douglas, Keanu Reeves, Liam Neeson, Jeff Bridges, Ralph Fiennes, Charlie Sheen, and Michael Keaton all reportedly turned down the role before Modine signed on to work with director Harlin.*

i) *Eddie Murphy is a suave nightclub owner tussling with the mob. Oh yeah, it's the year 2087, and his bar is on the moon.* Variety's *Peter Bart declared it "Instant Ishtar."*

We have had our own flops but never this high up on the seismic scale. Schadenfreude is the act of taking malicious pleasure from the misfortunes of others. It is considered poor manners. So take as little pleasure as possible, but as much encouragement as you can.

Answer Key:

a) *Howard the Duck* b) *Hudson Hawk* c) *Ishtar* d) *Battlefield Earth* e) *Cleopatra* f) *Heaven's Gate* g) *The Postman* h) *Cutthroat Island* i) *The Adventures of Pluto Nash* [3]

5. THE THESIS, THE NUGGET, AND THE EXTERNAL STORY

We are writing about characters. How do we discover them?

PEN'S CHARACTER PROVOKER

Try having some fun, and let your mind roam by asking yourself questions evoked by this checklist. I am calling it "Pen's Character Provoker". This is a work-in-progress for me. The concept is not necessarily to complete the whole list, but to see if any of the questions in the five areas of character open up your own understanding of who and what your characters might be.

For example: *How do my characters feel about their age? If they are from divorced parents, was this ugly and game-changing for them? If they are short, do they fight to compensate? etc.*

Get a notebook, engage each element in your mind. Play with it. See what it conjures.

---

[3]Edited from "Bombs Away!" by Kat Giantis. Special to MSN Movies *http://entertainment.msn.com/news/article.aspx?news=131054.*

THE PHYSICAL

Age/sex? _____

Height/weight/eyes? _____

Appearance/heredity/manner/posture/handicap? _____

_____

Tidy/untidy/unique points? _____

FAMILY

Ethnic background? Its status in character's life? Skin color/
nationality? What languages spoken? _____

_____

Social class/present status/Would like to be? _____

Position in family: orphan, single child, firstborn leader,
youngest spoiled? _____

Parents: happy, separated, divorced? _____

Father's career/mother's career? _____

Parents' beliefs, prejudices, fears, darkest secrets? _____

_____

RELATIONSHIPS WITH OPPOSITE SEX

Married, dating, single, divorced, has children/out of
wedlock? _____

Major love interest(s)? Compatible/incompatible? _____

Sexual preferences: heterosexual, homosexual? Hang-ups,
morals? _____

PERSONALITY / HOPES AND FEARS / PSYCHOLOGY

Whose deaths affected characters? _____

Was there a tragedy in the past? _____

What or who intruded on or abused them? _____

Good influences? Bad influences? _____

What kind of education? Intelligence level? _____

Favorite subjects/things hated? _____

Work or occupation: attitude to work. A slave? Wealthy and lazy? _____

Skills bank/abilities: adaptable to a new skill? Obsolete skills? _____

Hobby/project/objective? _____

Beliefs: religious, atheist, Zen, philosopher, spiritual? _____

Believes in luck? Scientist? Ethics or lack of? _____

Health: fitness to illness. Life expectancy? _____

Drugs: medical drugs, illegal? _____

Vices? _____

Hobbies, pastimes, sports? _____

Major emotional events in life: loss/gain, regret/success?
_____

Leader/follower? _____

Judge of character: gullible, astute, a Sherlock Homes? _____
_____

Entrepreneur? _____

Position in community? _____

Physical ambitions? _____

Emotional goals? _____

Politics? _____

Imagination: artistic/creative/inventions? _____
_____

CHARACTER FLAWS

Major personal obstacle (to overcome or be overcome by)?
_____

Shy? Introverted? Outgoing extrovert (with whom?) _____

Confident? Fear of failure? _____

Fears, phobias (from spiders to OCD)? _____

Secret in past (nugget material)? _____

Chief disappointment? _____

Pessimist, optimist, resigned, defeatist? _____

Sense of humor (or lack of)? _____

Fashion style (sloppy/fastidious)? _____

Dreamer procrastinator? _____

Driven, active militant? _____

Major outside hero influence (sports figure, superhero, famous real person)? _____

What books/literature heroes influenced by? The Bible? _Harry Potter_? _Time_ Magazine? Shakespeare? _____
_____

Who would they be if they could be someone else? _____

If they could be anywhere else, where? _____

Would describe self as _____

What characteristics emerge under pressure? _____

Relationship with animals? Pets? _____

Eccentricities? _____

What do they dream? What is in their nightmares? _____

What animal characteristics do they embody: elephant memory, slithery like a snake, loyal like a dog? _____

Actor or actress the character most resembles? _____

6. SOME CHARACTER TOOLS

Search history books, magazines, the Internet, and other sources for real-life examples of people — alive or historical — whose biographies and personality types excite you.

Use bi-association.

Combine wildly different traits from these people. See if you can create a complex, completely fictional character that impassions you to write about them.

7. VILLAINS

Lightheartedly, examine some well-known heroes or heroines, fictional or real. Find candidates who appeal to you, then add a streak of dark malevolence to them. (Bear in mind the human motives: greed, power, sex, vanity, etc.)

You are trying to create formidable fictional villains who are heroes to themselves. Perhaps a Steven Jobs type who believes he should use his computers to control people's minds, or a Winston Churchill persona who goes to war to prove he is still a potent leader and not an old man. Or consider a demented Joan of Arc–like young woman who takes up the sword to punish an English lover who spurned her.

These ideas may not be so far-fetched. Sadly, in rare cases, as our movie *Backdraft* pointed out, arsonists turn out to be firemen who relish the satisfaction of being adulated for fighting the fires they have created.

8. EDITING

Take a finished script of yours or something you are currently writing. Change the font (typestyle) and read the material. See if this helps you to see your material through fresh eyes and open up a sense of discovery and renewal.

Question yourself. Are you taking too many words to get your points across? Is your dialogue over long and obvious? Can you break into and out of scenes more economically? These discoveries can be exciting and surprisingly quick to change.

9. SELLING

Try to catch yourself in your daily life, the next time you consider engaging in an "error of omission," and do the opposite — instead, take that risk and try something positively daring!

Practice "commission." Doing this becomes easier, like riding a bicycle until it becomes second nature.

Write down every person's name you can think of who might be willing to write a recommendation for you. Phone the people on your list and let them know you are reading a screenwriting book that asks you to talk to your connections about your screenplay. See if they might be interested in reading your work.

10. PITCHING

Research potential target companies.

Consider their slate of films produced and movies listed in development, and try to assess as objectively as possible what kinds of questions they might ask about your project or script (how it matches against their past product, what stars you might cast, sum up possible poster lines, etc.). Can you find hit movies that relate to the style of films this company makes that could help frame your project in their terms of success?

When you have done your homework, brief a friend with this information and ask him or her to play the role of an executive who will be hearing your pitch and reviewing your project.

Go through the process of a meeting. Include greetings, give your pitch, and probe for questions generated by your material.

This kind of rehearsal can clarify what changes you should make in your approach and material before the real event. It can be a great confidence-builder.

11. UN-STARVING

Research someone you admire, whom you don't know personally. Write or call this person or persons and show them how much you know and care about their work and accomplishments, and then simply ask them for a little of their time to give advice on how they reached their goals. Explain that you would value their perspective on how they would approach the business today, if they were in your shoes. See where the conversation goes; it might be the beginning of a beautiful friendship.

12. TAKE SOME TIME TO CELEBRATE

Now you have made a sale and have a little money. Recharge your creative batteries. Take a little time to congratulate yourself. Do something fun and celebratory that feels like a reward, something familiar or something you've never done before! If you can, include the loved ones who have supported you.

13. A FILMMAKER'S "POSITIVE" THOUGHTS ON STRESS

Relax and aim for your goals.

When I was nineteen, I was idly inquisitive and bought a book on hypnosis. As I was reading a susceptibility test (a method used to evaluate a subject's responsiveness to suggestion), my left arm moved upward with the written suggestions. I had instant proof that hypnosis worked. Recently, scientists have used MRI studies and can tell that the human brain enters a different state when we are hypnotized. But they can't tell you much more than that.

In sports, it has been proven that internal visualization while in a resting state can improve our skills, and that we can reach a scientifically measurable state called "flow," in which athletes' skills and strengths seem to go on super autopilot, when they stop thinking and just "are." This state produces a higher caliber of play.

These studies made me curious whether artists could improve their skills and creativity this way. If we can imagine our goals, maybe we can send the thoughts to our unconscious to help guide us.

Over the years I discovered a simple relaxation technique that helped me unwind. It enables me to spend hassle-free time in my head thinking positive images aimed at reinforcing my personal objectives and helping to divorce me from stressful habits.

The method is like meditation.

Find a place to sit or lie down. Take a few very deep breaths. Close your eyes and start mentally going through your body, starting from your toes, and clench and relax each set of muscles. Ease up through your frame, tightening then relaxing each area: toes, arch of the foot, ankle, calf, knee, thigh, butt, belly, backbone, and upward. Breathe as shallowly as possible. Repeat the process a couple of times. My breathing can get to barely a whisper of air moving through my nose.

I believe that by deliberately making my physical self unwind, my unconscious mind becomes more receptive to positive suggestion. I try to program good ideas, healthy thoughts; I try to visualize places and goals I want to achieve for ten or twenty minutes. And sometimes, I just fall asleep!

It is hard to prove that I have changed my life or programmed my brain. Results don't suddenly switch themselves on. But I do feel that some suggested concepts have become seeded deep in my gray matter and have evolved to help me gain traction with my creativity and visualized goals. I believe I have helped myself reduce stress this way, too. I would put this in the category of: If it feels good to you, what the heck, give it a try.

Each to his or her own: Just changing your body chemistry may tune up your mood. Consider doing something wild and going to the nearest theme park and riding the rollercoasters for a few hours!

Chapter 17

HOW DO
YOU MEASURE
PASSION?

YOUR EFFORTS ARE MEANINGFUL TO YOU DESPITE OTHER PEOPLE'S OPINIONS

MOLL FLANDERS
Review from the *Tucson Weekly*
Directed by: Pen Densham

This marathon of a period movie, based loosely on the novel by Daniel Defoe, is plagued by a corny script and is just annoying in general. Moll Flanders (Robin Wright) is an 18th-century independent spirit, poor and alone, trying to make her way in the cold, hard world. It seems the only two choices she has are the convent and the whore-house, and she tries them both without much success. The dialogue in this movie is atrocious, as is the gut-wrenchingly dramatic plot. A special throne of badness is reserved here for the extremely annoying, other-worldly music that tortures the viewer subliminally for the first half of the movie. A few fine actors, including Stockard Channing, do their best to enliven this film, to no avail.

— Stacey Richter

Stacey has a right to her opinion. All movies will receive both good and bad criticism. *Moll* also had people who raved about it. As an artist, one must ignore both.

Moll was a personal test for me, supported by a massive number of caring people who contributed part of their lives to put my script on the screen. In my own opinion, I did the best I could. And I never knowingly let anyone down.

MGM graciously allowed me to dedicate the movie to my late mother. I consider writing and making the movie a privilege and one of the hardest, but best, experiences of my life.

The test: Knowing what I know now, would I do it again?

You are damn right I would!

Chapter **18**

FAMOUS LAST WORDS

When I'm asked a creative question as a director or as a writer, I'm always struck by the phenomenon that, although I fear I am going to ring empty like a hollow vessel, I often instantly have a definitive sense of the right answer. It's a certainty that I had no idea was in me until that very second, a super confidence-building feeling.

TRUST YOUR GUT INSTINCTS

Those little intuitions that you feel deep inside are usually the true knowing part of your psyche, and 90% of the time they guide you to the best course. You do know more than is in your direct consciousness. So...

Have as few "errors of omission" in your creative life as possible.

Be passionate — be daring — go forward.

ONLINE RESOURCES

There are dozens of great online resources for writers. Here are a few I think you may find useful:

ridingthealligator.com

scriptshark.com

mwp.com

writersstore.com

scriptmag.com

finaldraft.com

creativescreenwriting.com

writersbootcamp.com

austinfilmfestival.com

screenwritingexpo.com

GATOR GLOSSARY

In this book I reference some unique terms and phrases that I coined or used frequently, collaborating with my colleagues at Trilogy Entertainment Group. The reason for their existence is quite simple — at points, I needed each term to help me share a creative concept succinctly. You may already have your own approaches, or decide it is more helpful to invent your own, personal shorthand. Whatever the case, I present the ones found in *Riding the Alligator* as an easy reference.

A##hole Proofing: Making everything emphatically clear in your writing to ensure that you get your most important points across to lazy readers.

Accumulated Humiliations: The process by which a villain antagonist brings out and exploits the hero protagonist's weaknesses and failings of his or her nugget, until the hero finally throws off the load and rebounds to success.

Bi-association: The joining together of two old forms to create a new one.

Dream Receptors: A metaphor for my belief that our brains are designed to be receptive to movies, videos, and stories because they closely simulate the way that we perceive dreams.

The External Story: The "engine" of the movie that the audience is going to see, for example, an adventure, a romance, a thriller. Its real purpose is to test and change our character's nugget and attitudes as it evolves and entertains.

Framing Device: A good framing device is "an excuse with truth" that helps us feel more effective. It is a mental tool, angle, or approach created to confront new and intimidating goals successfully, such as cold-calling a stranger.

Fusion Writing: Unorthodox method of adding color into screenplay descriptions to make your work more compelling to readers. This may include writing dialogue or asides in descriptions to enhance your characters, or using more poetic language to capture the reader's imagination.

Getting Their Noses Out of the Popcorn: Putting a powerful, opening hook at the beginning of a movie or screenplay. Starting with a bang.

Hanging Words: One (or occasionally two) words in screenplay action lines or dialogue that hang over by themselves into the next line, making the reader's eyes work inefficiently hard.

Hiding the Medicine: The act of planting a subtle, but emotionally important lesson in a story that is not necessarily obvious to the reader/watcher, layered amid the more overt adventure and external discoveries.

Hiring the Promotable: Employing people with potential who harbor passion and a sense of direction, who want to learn and will work well with others.

Islands of Sanity: The main, few critical key events and story beats which propel the narrative and tend to coincide with Act Breaks and the story's major turning points. They act as landing points on the journey of writing the script.

Lewis and Clark: The idea that the first draft of a screenplay must be seen as an uncritical voyage of exploration, discovery, and creation. A few wrong turns must be expected when exploring unknown territory.

Life Scripts: Personal screenplays that are written intuitively from a powerful sense of inner vision. Often they are deeper and more originally voiced than scripts that are purely aimed to fit a mechanistic formula.

The Nugget: A simple, dark, and powerful life experience in a character's backstory that affects how he or she navigates emotionally, and also colors the character's approach to events and challenges.

Old Life Programs: The imperfect and incomplete modus operandi from a character's damaged, past experiences.

Orgasm: A whimsical term for a creative "climax" at a story's end. Utilizing the greatest character emotions and/or action elements to induce a powerful sense of completion.

Putting the Freeway Through: The editing phase after a first-draft screenplay of reviewing, deleting, and nipping and tucking the finished piece. Thus, keeping all the important elements but speeding up the read.

Raw Human: The final phase of the hero's becoming complete toward the end of a story, whereby heroes must soul-search and reinvent themselves in a hurry, into the character they "should" have been, if they have any hope to complete the story's quest.

The Ship in the Dock: The subjective and often incorrect assumption that another's completed, successful movie or career was free of the challenges that you might be facing with your own project.

Story Midwife: A friendly, caring reader who will encourage you through the pain of writing, without imposing personal agendas on you.

The Thesis: The spiritual purpose and moral compass of a story.

Van Gogh Syndrome: The by-product of creating something so unique it will not be understood or appreciated by those around you, and could be so artistically ahead of its time it that it is not recognized in the present.

ABOUT
THE AUTHOR

photo by *rwrightpix.com*

As a principal of Trilogy Entertainment Group, Pen Densham is an accomplished and award-winning writer-director-producer. His first job in show business was riding atop a live alligator for a theatrical short film made by his English parents. Pen decided to leave the school system at age fifteen, and has since spent his lifetime in the business of entertainment, selling films and television series, as well as hiring, mentoring, and collaborating with A-list writers along the way. Pen created the story for the revisionist *Robin Hood: Prince of Thieves* and co-wrote and produced the screenplay with his Trilogy partner John Watson. He wrote and directed *Moll Flanders* for MGM, as well as writing and directing *Houdini* for TNT.

Pen and Trilogy have produced fourteen feature films and worked with talent like Jay Baruchel, Jeff Bridges, Bill Murray, Morgan Freeman, Ron Howard, Kevin Costner, Sylvester Stallone, Norman Jewison, Jodie Foster, Emile Hirsch, Mark Ruffalo, Johnathon Schaech, and Robin Wright. Pen is proud to have personally revived both *The Outer Limits* and *The Twilight Zone* franchises for their return to television, and was named the eighth most powerful person in Science Fiction by *Cinefantastique* magazine. Pen is also an adjunct professor at the University of Southern California's prestigious School of Cinematic Arts. He is also a visiting filmmaker at the Canadian Film Centre in Toronto.

Pen lives in Los Angeles, California with his wife, Wendy Savage. They have a son, Nevin, also a writer, and daughter, Victoria who plans on teaching. Pen makes it a point to visit his relatives in Canada, England, and Australia as often as he can. He has had no close encounters with any alligators recently.

Contact: *ridingthealligator.com*

SAVE THE CAT!®
THE LAST BOOK ON
SCREENWRITING YOU'LL EVER NEED!

BLAKE SNYDER

He's made millions of dollars selling screenplays to Hollywood and now screenwriter Blake Snyder tells all. "Save the Cat!®" is just one of Snyder's many ironclad rules for making your ideas more marketable and your script more satisfying — and saleable, including:
- The four elements of every winning logline.
- The seven immutable laws of screenplay physics.
- The 10 genres and why they're important to your movie.
- Why your Hero must serve your idea.
- Mastering the Beats.
- Mastering the Board to create the Perfect Beast.
- How to get back on track with ironclad and proven rules for script repair.

This ultimate insider's guide reveals the secrets that none dare admit, told by a show biz veteran who's proven that you can sell your script if you can save the cat.

"Imagine what would happen in a town where more writers approached screenwriting the way Blake suggests? My weekend read would dramatically improve, both in sellable/producible content and in discovering new writers who understand the craft of storytelling and can be hired on assignment for ideas we already have in house."
> – From the Foreword by Sheila Hanahan Taylor, Vice President, Development at Zide/Perry Entertainment, whose films include *American Pie, Cats and Dogs, Final Destination*

"One of the most comprehensive and insightful how-to's out there. Save the Cat!® is a must-read for both the novice and the professional screenwriter."
> – Todd Black, Producer, *The Pursuit of Happyness, The Weather Man, S.W.A.T, Alex and Emma, Antwone Fisher*

"Want to know how to be a successful writer in Hollywood? The answers are here. Blake Snyder has written an insider's book that's informative — and funny, too."
> – David Hoberman, Producer, *The Shaggy Dog* (2005), *Raising Helen, Walking Tall, Bringing Down the House, Monk* (TV)

BLAKE SNYDER, besides selling million-dollar scripts to both Disney and Spielberg, was one of Hollywood's most successful spec screenwriters. Blake's vision continues on *www.blakesnyder.com*.

$19.95 · 216 PAGES · ORDER NUMBER 34RLS · ISBN: 9781932907001

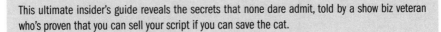

24 HOURS | **1.800.833.5738** | **WWW.MWP.COM**

THE WRITER'S JOURNEY – 3RD EDITION
MYTHIC STRUCTURE FOR WRITERS

CHRISTOPHER VOGLER

BEST SELLER
OVER 180,000 COPIES SOLD!

See why this book has become an international best seller and a true classic. *The Writer's Journey* explores the powerful relationship between mythology and storytelling in a clear, concise style that's made it required reading for movie executives, screenwriters, playwrights, scholars, and fans of pop culture all over the world.

Both fiction and nonfiction writers will discover a set of useful myth-inspired storytelling paradigms (i.e., "The Hero's Journey") and step-by-step guidelines to plot and character development. Based on the work of Joseph Campbell, *The Writer's Journey* is a must for all writers interested in further developing their craft.

The updated and revised third edition provides new insights and observations from Vogler's ongoing work on mythology's influence on stories, movies, and man himself.

"This book is like having the smartest person in the story meeting come home with you and whisper what to do in your ear as you write a screenplay. Insight for insight, step for step, Chris Vogler takes us through the process of connecting theme to story and making a script come alive."
> – Lynda Obst, Producer, *Sleepless in Seattle, How to Lose a Guy in 10 Days*;
> Author, *Hello, He Lied*

"This is a book about the stories we write, and perhaps more importantly, the stories we live. It is the most influential work I have yet encountered on the art, nature, and the very purpose of storytelling."
> – Bruce Joel Rubin, Screenwriter, *Stuart Little 2, Deep Impact,*
> *Ghost, Jacob's Ladder*

CHRISTOPHER VOGLER is a veteran story consultant for major Hollywood film companies and a respected teacher of filmmakers and writers around the globe. He has influenced the stories of movies from *The Lion King* to *Fight Club* to *The Thin Red Line* and most recently wrote the first installment of *Ravenskull*, a Japanese-style manga or graphic novel. He is the executive producer of the feature film *P.S. Your Cat is Dead* and writer of the animated feature *Jester Till*.

$26.95 · 448 PAGES · ORDER NUMBER 76RLS · ISBN: 9781932907360

SELLING YOUR STORY IN 60 SECONDS
THE GUARANTEED WAY TO GET
YOUR SCREENPLAY OR NOVEL READ

MICHAEL HAUGE

BEST SELLER

Best-selling author Michael Hauge reveals:
- How to Design, Practice, and Present the 60-Second Pitch
- The Cardinal Rule of Pitching
- The 10 Key Components of a Commercial Story
- The 8 Steps to a Powerful Pitch
- Targeting Your Buyers
- Securing Opportunities to Pitch
- Pitching Templates
- And much more, including "The Best Pitch I Ever Heard," an exclusive collection from major film executives

"Michael Hauge's principles and methods are so well argued that the mysteries of effective screenwriting can be understood — even by directors."

> — Phillip Noyce, Director, *Patriot Games, Clear and Present Danger, The Quiet American, Rabbit-Proof Fence*

"... one of the few authentically good teachers out there. Every time I revisit my notes, I learn something new or reinforce something that I need to remember."

> — Jeff Arch, Screenwriter, *Sleepless in Seattle, Iron Will*

"Michael Hauge's method is magic — but unlike most magicians, he shows you how the trick is done."

> — William Link, Screenwriter & Co-Creator, *Columbo; Murder, She Wrote*

"By following the formula we learned in Michael Hauge's seminar, we got an agent, optioned our script, and now have a three-picture deal at Disney."

> — Paul Hoppe and David Henry, Screenwriters

MICHAEL HAUGE is the author of *Writing Screenplays That Sell*, now in its 30th printing, and has presented his seminars and lectures to more than 30,000 writers and filmmakers. He has coached hundreds of screenwriters and producers on their screenplays and pitches, and has consulted on projects for Warner Brothers, Disney, New Line, CBS, Lifetime, Julia Roberts, Jennifer Lopez, Kirsten Dunst, and Morgan Freeman.

$12.95 · 150 PAGES · ORDER NUMBER 64RLS · ISBN: 9781932907209

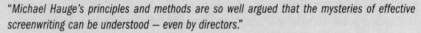

24 HOURS | 1.800.833.5738 | WWW.MWP.COM

{ THE MYTH OF MWP }

In a dark time, a light bringer came along, leading the curious and the frustrated to clarity and empowerment. It took the well-guarded secrets out of the hands of the few and made them available to all. It spread a spirit of openness and creative freedom, and built a storehouse of knowledge dedicated to the betterment of the arts.

The essence of the Michael Wiese Productions (MWP) is empowering people who have the burning desire to express themselves creatively. We help them realize their dreams by putting the tools in their hands. We demystify the sometimes secretive worlds of screenwriting, directing, acting, producing, film financing, and other media crafts.

By doing so, we hope to bring forth a realization of 'conscious media' which we define as being positively charged, emphasizing hope and affirming positive values like trust, cooperation, self-empowerment, freedom, and love. Grounded in the deep roots of myth, it aims to be healing both for those who make the art and those who encounter it. It hopes to be transformative for people, opening doors to new possibilities and pulling back veils to reveal hidden worlds.

MWP has built a storehouse of knowledge unequaled in the world, for no other publisher has so many titles on the media arts. Please visit www.mwp.com where you will find many free resources and a 25% discount on our books. Sign up and become part of the wider creative community!

Onward and upward,

Michael Wiese
Publisher/Filmmaker

FILM & VIDEO BOOKS

TO RECEIVE A FREE MWP NEWSLETTER, CLICK ON WWW.MWP.COM TO REGISTER

SCREENWRITING | WRITING

And the Best Screenplay Goes to... | Dr. Linda Seger | $26.95
Archetypes for Writers | Jennifer Van Bergen | $22.95
Bali Brothers | Lacy Waltzman, Matthew Bishop, Michael Wiese | $12.95
Cinematic Storytelling | Jennifer Van Sijll | $24.95
Could It Be a Movie? | Christina Hamlett | $26.95
Creating Characters | Marisa D'Vari | $26.95
Crime Writer's Reference Guide, The | Martin Roth | $20.95
Deep Cinema | Mary Trainor-Brigham | $19.95
Elephant Bucks | Sheldon Bull | $24.95
Fast, Cheap & Written That Way | John Gaspard | $26.95
Hollywood Standard – 2nd Edition, The | Christopher Riley | $18.95
Horror Screenwriting | Devin Watson | $24.95
I Could've Written a Better Movie than That! | Derek Rydall | $26.95
Inner Drives | Pamela Jaye Smith | $26.95
Moral Premise, The | Stanley D. Williams, Ph.D. | $24.95
Myth and the Movies | Stuart Voytilla | $26.95
Power of the Dark Side, The | Pamela Jaye Smith | $22.95
Psychology for Screenwriters | William Indick, Ph.D. | $26.95
Reflections of the Shadow | Jeffrey Hirschberg | $26.95
Rewrite | Paul Chitlik | $16.95
Romancing the A-List | Christopher Keane | $18.95
Save the Cat! | Blake Snyder | $19.95
Save the Cat! Goes to the Movies | Blake Snyder | $24.95
Screenwriting 101 | Neill D. Hicks | $16.95
Screenwriting for Teens | Christina Hamlett | $18.95
Script-Selling Game, The | Kathie Fong Yoneda | $16.95
Stealing Fire From the Gods, 2nd Edition | James Bonnet | $26.95
Talk the Talk | Penny Penniston | $24.95
Way of Story, The | Catherine Ann Jones | $22.95
What Are You Laughing At? | Brad Schreiber | $19.95
Writer's Journey – 3rd Edition, The | Christopher Vogler | $26.95
Writer's Partner, The | Martin Roth | $24.95
Writing the Action Adventure Film | Neill D. Hicks | $14.95
Writing the Comedy Film | Stuart Voytilla & Scott Petri | $14.95
Writing the Killer Treatment | Michael Halperin | $14.95
Writing the Second Act | Michael Halperin | $19.95
Writing the Thriller Film | Neill D. Hicks | $14.95
Writing the TV Drama Series, 2nd Edition | Pamela Douglas | $26.95
Your Screenplay Sucks! | William M. Akers | $19.95

FILMMAKING

Film School | Richard D. Pepperman | $24.95
Power of Film, The | Howard Suber | $27.95

PITCHING

Perfect Pitch – 2nd Edition, The | Ken Rotcop | $19.95
Selling Your Story in 60 Seconds | Michael Hauge | $12.95

SHORTS

Filmmaking for Teens, 2nd Edition | Troy Lanier & Clay Nichols | $24.95
Making It Big in Shorts | Kim Adelman | $22.95

BUDGET | PRODUCTION MANAGEMENT

Film & Video Budgets, 5th Updated Edition | Deke Simon | $26.95
Film Production Management 101 | Deborah S. Patz | $39.95

DIRECTING | VISUALIZATION

Animation Unleashed | Ellen Besen | $26.95

Cinematography for Directors | Jacqueline Frost | $29.95
Citizen Kane Crash Course in Cinematography | David Worth | $19.95
Directing Actors | Judith Weston | $26.95
Directing Feature Films | Mark Travis | $26.95
Fast, Cheap & Under Control | John Gaspard | $26.95
Film Directing: Cinematic Motion, 2nd Edition | Steven D. Katz | $27.95
Film Directing: Shot by Shot | Steven D. Katz | $27.95
Film Director's Intuition, The | Judith Weston | $26.95
First Time Director | Gil Bettman | $27.95
From Word to Image, 2nd Edition | Marcie Begleiter | $26.95
I'll Be in My Trailer! | John Badham & Craig Modderno | $26.95
Master Shots | Christopher Kenworthy | $24.95
Setting Up Your Scenes | Richard D. Pepperman | $24.95
Setting Up Your Shots, 2nd Edition | Jeremy Vineyard | $22.95
Working Director, The | Charles Wilkinson | $22.95

DIGITAL | DOCUMENTARY | SPECIAL

Digital Filmmaking 101, 2nd Edition | Dale Newton & John Gaspard | $26.95
Digital Moviemaking 3.0 | Scott Billups | $24.95
Digital Video Secrets | Tony Levelle | $26.95
Greenscreen Made Easy | Jeremy Hanke & Michele Yamazaki | $19.95
Producing with Passion | Dorothy Fadiman & Tony Levelle | $22.95
Special Effects | Michael Slone | $31.95

EDITING

Cut by Cut | Gael Chandler | $35.95
Cut to the Chase | Bobbie O'Steen | $24.95
Eye is Quicker, The | Richard D. Pepperman | $27.95
Film Editing | Gael Chandler | $34.95
Invisible Cut, The | Bobbie O'Steen | $28.95

SOUND | DVD | CAREER

Complete DVD Book, The | Chris Gore & Paul J. Salamoff | $26.95
Costume Design 101, 2nd Edition | Richard La Motte | $24.95
Hitting Your Mark, 2nd Edition | Steve Carlson | $22.95
Sound Design | David Sonnenschein | $19.95
Sound Effects Bible, The | Ric Viers | $26.95
Storyboarding 101 | James Fraioli | $19.95
There's No Business Like Soul Business | Derek Rydall | $22.95
You Can Act! | D. W. Brown | $24.95

FINANCE | MARKETING | FUNDING

Art of Film Funding, The | Carole Lee Dean | $26.95
Bankroll | Tom Malloy | $26.95
Complete Independent Movie Marketing Handbook, The | Mark Steven Bosko | $39.95
Getting the Money | Jeremy Jusso | $26.95
Independent Film and Videomakers Guide – 2nd Edition, The | Michael Wiese | $29.95
Independent Film Distribution | Phil Hall | $26.95
Shaking the Money Tree, 3rd Edition | Morrie Warshawski | $26.95

MEDITATION | ART

Mandalas of Bali | Dewa Nyoman Batuan | $39.95

OUR FILMS

Dolphin Adventures: DVD | Michael Wiese and Hardy Jones | $24.95
Hardware Wars: DVD | Written and Directed by Ernie Fosselius | $14.95
On the Edge of a Dream | Michael Wiese | $16.95
Sacred Sites of the Dalai Lamas– DVD, The | Documentary by Michael Wiese | $24.95